The Normans in Britain

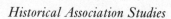

The Normans
1066-1154

Wm
The Conqueror m Matilda
of Flanders
1066-1087

Wm II
1087-1100

Adela
m Stephen

Henry I m Edith
1100-1135   daughter of
Macolm III
of Scotland

Stephen m Matilda
1135-1154   of Boulogne

(1) Henry V
Emp of
Germany
(d 1125

Matilda m Geoffrey
(d 1167)   Count of
Anjou
(d 1151)

Henry II
1154-1189

B

Historical Association Studies

General Editors: Muriel Chamberlain and H. T. Dickinson

The Historical Association, founded in 1906, brings together people who share an interest in, and love for, the past. It aims to further the study and teaching of history at all levels: teacher and student, amateur and professional. This is one of over 100 publications available at preferential rates to members. Membership also includes journals at generous discounts and gives access to courses, conferences, tours and regional and local activities. Full details are available from The Secretary, The Historical Association, 59a Kennington Park Road, London SE11 4JH, telephone: 071-735 3901.

The Normans in Britain

David Walker

BLACKWELL
Oxford UK & Cambridge USA

The right of David Walker to be identified as author of this work has been asserted in accordance with the Copyright, Designs and Patents Act 1988.

First published 1995

Blackwell Publishers, the publishing imprint of Basil Blackwell Ltd
108 Cowley Road
Oxford OX4 1JF
UK

Basil Blackwell Inc.
238 Main Street
Cambridge, Massachusetts 02142
USA

British Library Cataloguing in Publication Data
A CIP catalogue record for this book is available from the British Library.

Library of Congress Cataloging-in-Publication Data
Walker, David, 1923–
      The Normans in Britain / David Walker.
          p.   cm. – (Historical Association studies)
      Includes bibliographical references and index.
       ISBN 0-631-19693-5. – ISBN 0-631-18582-8 (pbk.)
        1. Great Britain – History – Norman period, 1066–1154.   2. Normans – Great Britain – History.   I. Title.   II. Series.
      DA195.W35   1995
      942.02 – dc20   94-28142
                                                                                                                    CIP

Typeset in 11 on 13 pt Ehrhardt by Best-set Typesetter Ltd., Hong Kong
Printed in Great Britain by Hartnolls Limited, Bodmin, Cornwall

This book is printed on acid-free paper

Contents

Maps

Preface

My aim in this book has been to introduce readers to a wide theme of Norman expansion and to survey the main characteristics of Norman penetration and settlement in different regions of Britain. My own interest in this theme has been reflected in earlier publications on feudal society in England and the Welsh Marches and on medieval Wales. I have examined Norman influence in Ireland and Scotland and the spread of Romanesque architecture in lectures and seminars; my interest in these fields was given focus, many years ago, by Professor Lewis Warren's invitation to take part in a series of lectures on Norman expansion at The Queen's University, Belfast. The period I have adopted for England and Wales runs from 1066 to 1216; for Scotland and Ireland the upper limit must be placed somewhat later, about 1240. In each country, some themes emerge long before the arrival of Norman settlers.

There has been much debate about the proper national or racial descriptions to be used in this context: Norman, Anglo-Norman, English and other variants. The further settlers are removed from a Norman background, the more difficult it is to express subtle gradations. As nouns, used to identify people, such forms as Anglo-Norman, Cambro-Norman and Hibernico-Norman have very little meaning. I have used Anglo-Norman as an adjective; it describes influences exerted in Wales and Scotland with some accuracy. With reservations, I have retained Anglo-Norman for Ireland; by 1170 the hybrid term is far from satisfactory, but it is by no means outmoded where concepts of law, society, military tactics and ethos are concerned.

The primary purpose of references to works in the bibliography is to guide readers who may, as I hope, wish to explore these themes in greater depth. I hope that, limited as they are, the references may also serve to indicate my debt to many scholars who have written on Anglo-Norman history. Chapter 6 depends very largely on many visits which my wife and I have made to castles, churches and other sites in France and throughout the British Isles, and on an extensive collection of detailed architectural studies and scholarly guides.

I am grateful to Dr Marjorie Chibnall for her helpful advice and perceptive comments in the preparation of this book and to my wife, Margaret. The maps have been produced by Guy Lewis, the senior cartographer in the Department of Geography at the University of Wales, Swansea. To plot all the places named in this book would require more than four basic maps, so for each country I have tried to indicate the most important centres and a cross-section of the lesser sites, castles, towns and religious houses, difficult though the problems of selection have been. I am also grateful to Tessa Harvey for her care in seeing this book through the press.

I acknowledge with gratitude grants from the Isla Johnson Trust and from the Archdeacon Bevan Memorial Fund.

David Walker
Swansea

1

The Norman Impact

The Norman invasion of England in the autumn of 1066 and the subsequent conquest of the kingdom was a major element in Norman expansion in Europe in the eleventh century. The establishment of a new order in England, which introduced sweeping changes in the country's political, social and economic life, had long-term consequences for the rest of Britain. Norman advances into Wales began very early, well before the Normans were secure in England itself. Norman influences were affecting the church in Ireland before the end of the Conqueror's reign, though military invasion and conquest, occasionally hinted as a possibility, did not materialize until 1169. Meanwhile, by a very different process, Norman influence became a crucial factor in the development of the Scottish kingdom.

While English medievalists usually treat these as national themes in isolation, Barrow (1956) and Davies (1990) study them as a unity. Here I have tried to present a broad survey of Norman expansion in Britain, with separate chapters devoted to England and its Celtic neighbours, each illustrating different facets of Norman expansion.

Some issues require a more generalized analysis. The decisive nature of the events of September and October 1066 is the basis for Norman rule and Norman expansion. Much turned on the expertise of the Norman forces in the eleventh and twelfth centuries. The Norman kings and their Angevin successors had a strong sense of legitimacy. England had been won by appeal to arms, but at Hastings the Conqueror gained what he regarded as lawfully his. The same theme emerges in Ireland in the 1170s, and it is a recurrent feature in Wales and Scotland. Finally, faced with the interpretation both of Norman settlement in England and of Anglo-Norman settlements in Wales and Ireland, as well as the assessment of Anglo-Norman influence in Scotland, historians have been moving towards explanations that have much in common. Already clearly marked out as long ago as the 1960s, 'colonialism' and 'exploitation' have become common currency, especially in the work of Irish, Welsh and Scottish historians, where they have been made a dominant theme.

The Norman conquest of England was planned and undertaken as a matter of ducal policy. From a Norman point of view, given literary expression before 1071 by William of Poitiers, the whole enterprise was designed to secure the kingdom and so to justify Duke William's claims to the English throne. It could be presented as an appeal to the ordeal of battle through which the judgement of God might be established. At the battle of Hastings that was achieved, and the lawful claimant to the throne was vindicated. Such a view was an over-simplification, but it is the basic theme of the Bayeux Tapestry. That there were a number of claimants to the Confessor's throne and that the process of conquest was long and slow were factors either not recognized or allowed to fall into the background. In the immediate aftermath of William's accession the principle of legitimacy had prevailed. In the Anglo-Saxon Chronicle the Conqueror's claim was never expressed in such terms: there, as it appeared, England was being punished for its sins.

The consequence of the Norman thesis was that the new king was concerned to establish his authority over the kingdom that Edward the Confessor had ruled. Apart from problems of defence, what might happen beyond its boundaries was not a matter of immediate concern. In fact, the process of conquest was long and slow. There were a number of claimants to the English throne who were only gradually removed from the scene. Wales might be a source of strength for disaffected magnates in the midlands, and Scotland a place of refuge for the Confessor's kindred and for

English magnates who would not accept Norman rule. William governed his kingdom as lawful king, strengthening his hold on distant regions, distributing English lands as rewards for his continental supporters, and putting a stamp of legality on both the acquisition and the use of English lordships. At the end of his reign, he was enquiring with much curiosity and perhaps some bewilderment about questions of tenure. But if he and his administrators had lost sight of the detail, they had not compromised the main principles, that what his men held they should hold lawfully, and that if there were disputes these should be settled by law. The Norman conquest of England was not a smash-and-grab raid: it was not a free-for-all in which great magnates and fighting men of lesser status could take what they would and hold it without challenge.

How could invasion and conquest come about? The critical problem for the English kingdom was that King Edward was childless. Returning to England in 1042 in middle age, after a long exile, he depended heavily on Godwine, earl of Wessex; if Godwine was not king-maker, he was determined to keep the new ruler firmly under his own control. As one means of achieving that, the king was married to Godwine's daughter Edith, and for nineteen years they survived a political marriage. Once, in 1051, Edward threw off the constraining influence of Godwine and his family and set aside his wife, but he could not turn a temporary reverse into a permanent victory, and the family swept back into power the following year. In practical terms, Edward could not discard Edith in the hope of providing a direct heir through another marriage. It was a certainty that his kingdom would not pass to a son, and he had therefore to make formal arrangements for the future.

Edward's exile had been spent with his kinsmen in Normandy. When he became king he turned naturally to Normandy for companions and advisers to join him in the kingdom. He also looked to the ducal family for a successor. In 1051 he promised the throne to Duke William and gained the approval of leading English magnates; and despite later shifts in policy he sent his most influential adviser, Harold, by then earl of Wessex, to Normandy to confirm the promise. His visit was probably made in 1064, though a case has been argued for the autumn of 1065. At an earlier stage, in 1057, another prospective successor was brought back to England. He was the Confessor's closest heir by direct male descent – Edward the Atheling, son of the Confessor's half-brother, King Edmund Ironside. Edward and his family had lived in exile in eastern Europe since 1016. He died within a few weeks of his return, but he had brought with him his wife, his son Edgar the Atheling and his daughters Margaret and Christina, who were to play important roles in English, Scottish and Anglo-Norman politics.

Beyond those who were unquestionably linked with the king by ties of blood there were other claimants. The queen's brothers, Tostig and Harold, were within the royal circle, and each was influential. Earl Harold governed as a *sub-regulus* in all but name, while Tostig was responsible for the turbulent earldom of Northumbria and was a favourite companion and adviser of the ageing king. Tostig's sister regarded him with special favour and was personally involved in intrigue and political murder on his behalf. In 1065 he was challenged and driven out of Northumbria, and he believed that Harold was directly responsible for this disaster. It turned him into an implacable enemy, and he went into exile determined to seek restitution if not vengeance.

At this critical stage Edgar's claims were set aside and the promise to Duke William was ignored. As the old king lay dying, he designated Earl Harold as his successor. The Bayeux Tapestry depicts the scene without comment. Norman apologists made no attempt to refute the claim. In great haste Harold was crowned. His hopes of commanding loyalty throughout the kingdom were not strong: in the north he was accepted largely through the influence of Wulfstan, bishop of Worcester, while in the midlands he strengthened the links between himself and the two brothers Edwin earl of Mercia and Morcar earl of Northumbria by marrying their sister. Already in the forefront of English politics, they were brought within the royal circle by this marriage.

In the background there was another claim to the succession, which posed a long-term threat to the security of the English kingdom. In 1038 Harthacnut and Magnus of Norway came to

I prepared some slideshow with

... paper. Now my show today they

you sent me that anyway they

were paper. :)

terms and agreed that when one of them died the survivor should succeed to his lands in the north. Harthacnut was not at that stage king of England, but when he died in 1042 Magnus and his successors understood the agreement to cover the English kingdom. At intervals during the Confessor's reign and again in 1066 this claim was the justification for Norwegian attacks on England.

The result of these claims was that in 1066 Magnus's heir, Harold Hardraada of Norway was planning to overthrow King Harold in England; Duke William was actively organizing his invasion of the kingdom; Earl Tostig was looking for allies with whom he might stage a return to the English political scene. Edgar the Atheling was too young to be scheming for himself, but was a useful pawn for others to use. Edwin and Morcar might swing the balance in any critical encounter but were lukewarm in their support of King Harold.

When Norman writers identified the battle for England as a battle between the duke as rightful claimant and the king as a perjurer and usurper, they were oversimplifying a complex problem. King Harold, on his part, recognized the Norman threat as the essential problem, and he geared his military preparations to check and defeat an invasion from Normandy. Throughout the early summer the duke was building a fleet of transport ships and mustering an army drawn from Normandy and the neighbouring French lordships, while Harold concentrated on the defence of the Channel coast. In May, Earl Tostig made an abortive attempt to attack England, and that, as it seems, prompted what proved to be a premature mobilization of English forces. Tostig was repulsed and no major invasion occurred, but the English forces had to face the full summer under arms. In the early autumn the strain of long mobilization and of stormy weather in the Channel forced Harold to withdraw his naval forces, and his army began to disperse. Then, in mid-September, Harold Hardraada, with Earl Tostig, landed in the north and attacked York. The northern earls withstood him at Fulford Gate but they were eventually defeated with heavy losses. King Harold moved swiftly and by forced marches took his army to the north, surprised the Norwegians and overwhelmed them at

Stamford Bridge. Harold Hardraada and Tostig died in the battle, and a small remnant of their army – less than a tenth – was allowed to make its way back to Norway.

How far, it may be asked, did these two battles affect the balance of military resources between the English and the Normans? Any attempt to estimate the size of the armies commanded by Edwin and Morcar at Fulford or by King Harold at Stamford Bridge must, at best, be tentative. For the country as a whole Domesday assessments can be used to suggest approximate figures on the basis that five hides could sustain a fighting man and that six carucates was probably the equivalent unit in eastern and northern England. Kent, and probably Sussex, fall outside the normal pattern, and Northumberland, Durham and a large part of Lancashire were not included in the survey. So, with reservations, that would suggest a military potential of about 13,000 men, and when allowance has been made for the northern territories and for a small number of mercenary fighters, the total is likely to be nearer to 14,000. Edwin and Morcar could have called upon a maximum of between 4,300 and 5,000 men, and the lands controlled by King Harold and his family and by Earl Waltheof may have produced about 9,000 men. Whether more than 70 per cent of these would have turned out even in a major emergency (as one commentator has suggested) is simply a matter of guesswork. Harold's army was certainly below maximum strength, since his forces were being disbanded when he made the decision to march north to meet the Scandinavians.

The casualties suffered in the two northern battles cannot be assessed. At Fulford the task of the English forces was to deny the Norwegians access to York; after a long and vigorous defence they were overwhelmed, and their losses must have been heavy, especially in the later stages of the battle. At Stamford Bridge, where Harold had the benefit of surprise, the Norwegian casualties were very heavy and English losses much smaller. When Harold marched south to confront Duke William his army may have included many who had been wounded at Stamford Bridge, but he was not leading a bedraggled and ineffective force; he still commanded an army whose morale was high. Stamford Bridge was fought on 25 September. By 6 October Harold was in London. Five days later he began to move his troops towards the south coast, and before dusk on 13 October Duke William was made aware that his enemy was within easy striking distance of his base at Hastings. William of Poitiers recorded the information – should we call it fact? – that a Norman already settled in England, Robert son of Guimara, sent a message to Duke William that Harold had just defeated Harold Hardraada and would soon send the Norman duke back to his duchy, so perhaps he would be wise to set sail for home before disaster overtook him. William of Poitiers was determined to show that the duke would have no fear, however great the odds against him. The enemy was still formidable. Historians have criticized Harold's judgement to march against the Normans with such haste. There were reserves which might have strengthened his army, including the survivors of the northern earldoms once they had had the chance to regroup. We do not know how far he had been able to mobilize forces from southern England in the sixteen days between the battle of Stamford Bridge and his departure from London. With all these uncertainties, he was still able to muster an army of about 7,000 men. One of his great weaknesses at Hastings was that he had very few archers with him, and the assumption is often made that he moved away from London before a reasonable complement of archers could join him. But at least his army was not inferior in numbers to the Norman duke's forces and it could hold at bay all the Norman assaults for a long day's battle. Three factors may lie behind Harold's decision to press on with his attack. His particular style as a commander was the effective use of a swift advance and a surprise attack. His political position was weak and delay might not be to his advantage. And he was under pressure from the Normans: Duke William was deliberately raiding and harassing Harold's estates to draw the king south.

In the event, surprise was not possible. Both commanders were anxious for a quick engagement. Duke William's army moved out from Hastings early in the morning of 14 October. King Harold, confronted by the Normans, took up a defensive position along a barren escarpment, and the Normans, eager for battle, were attacking him before his army was completely in position. Numerically, the two armies appear to have been well matched. The battle was long and hard, and the inference is that neither army had the advantage of greatly superior numbers. Harold is thought to have had 6,000 or 7,000 men: we do not know the balance between trained fighting men, his thegns and housecarls, and peasant militia. His lack of archers certainly gave the Normans an advantage. Duke William is thought to have had some 2,000 knights (though some estimates are as high as 3,000), with 4,000 or 5,000 support troops, infantry, archers and, probably, crossbowmen.

The most influential of recent discussions about the battle, by Allen Brown (1981) and John Gillingham (1989), which originally had a very limited circulation, have been reprinted in *Anglo-Norman Warfare* (Strickland, 1992). Brown questions Harold's gifts as a commander, emphasizes the strength of the professional element in the English army and hints at the contribution, which may have been substantial, made by Duke William's infantry. Gillingham explores the making of the Conqueror as a military commander and sets the battle in a wider context of European warfare.

For the Normans the tactical challenge was to sustain attacks up a short but sharp incline and to break through the English defences. Their archers could weaken the English, but the only way the English could be defeated was by penetrating their ranks and destroying the elite forces in close combat. That individual knights had broken through, long before the closing stages of the battle, is made clear in the Bayeux Tapestry. Harold's brothers, Leofwine and Gyrth, were killed; the artist shows Norman knights penetrating the English defence and cutting down both of the earls. For much of the day the English repulsed Norman attacks and maintained their defence. As the Normans fell back – at times with great loss and much confusion – their commanders had to restore order. At one point the rumour spread that Duke William had been killed; he had to lift his helmet and gallop through the mêlée to reassure his troops and restore confidence. Young men, not yet knights, had to be turned back into battle by the duke's brother Odo, bishop of Bayeux.

As the day lengthened, the Normans began to gain the advantage. A critical factor was the degree to which discipline could be imposed upon the whole army, or utilized by smaller contingents to sway the course of the battle. Certainly, squadrons of knights could use on the battlefield the tactics they had mastered as part of their training. With the Norman forces in disorder, English troops broke ranks to pursue them, but under William's direction the Norman cavalry rallied and surrounded and destroyed them. In 'feigned flights', contingents retreated in apparent confusion, tempting groups of peasant militia to pursue them. Careful drilling made it possible for the Normans to turn in good order and charge down the infantry exposed to their attack. The device was said to have been used twice in the course of the battle.

As the afternoon wore on, with the English forces much depleted, Duke William mounted another major attack deploying his archers, knights and, it seems, infantry, in a show of strength. Eventually, the Normans could penetrate right through to the point where Harold still stood, with his dragon standard close by. The Bayeux Tapestry portrays the scene vividly: the standard was thrown down, the king's bodyguard was slaughtered and Harold, wounded but still fighting, was cut down by a Norman knight. Those English troops which survived moved away into the dusk seeking cover in the wild country to the north. Some of them turned in a last act of defiance and inflicted further losses on their pursuers. But it was the English who suffered casualties on an overwhelming scale. William of Poitiers noted with pride that some of the most famous Norman fighters of their day died at Hastings, but in the carnage of the battle the flower of the nobility and the youth of England had perished.

How the Normans capitalized on their victory and, by a slow process, extended their control over the greater part of the English kingdom is an important theme, which is examined in depth in chapter 2. Here it must be said that the battle established in fact the claims made by Duke William as the lawful successor to Edward the Confessor. Harold, consistently belittled by Norman apologists, was presented as the perjured vassal properly and justly overthrown: in the language of a later age he might be considered the pretender.

Beyond the boundaries of the English kingdom the Normans did not assert the principle of legitimacy in such overt terms. In Wales the earliest advances were made by baronial initiative, and a pattern of piecemeal acquisition was established which marked the political structure of Wales until the Acts of Union of 1536 and 1542. Royal influence was exerted at an early date. In Domesday Book, Rhys ap Tewdwr of Deheubarth and Robert of Rhuddlan in Gwynedd paid King William £40 a year, and the revenues of the castleries of Strigoil and Caerleon were paid by royal officials. William Rufus encouraged new advances into the Welsh kingdoms of Brycheiniog and Morgannwg, and under his patronage a new generation of Norman lords was established in Welsh territory. Henry I made claims that were wider and more explicit. Rees Davies (1985) has argued with force that he intervened in Welsh affairs more than any other English king before Edward I. He destroyed the house of Bellême with direct consequences for south-west Wales. Pembrokeshire was administered by royal officials, and at Carmarthen another royal official, Walter of Gloucester, was active on the king's behalf. Under Henry's patronage new and powerful Norman families were introduced into Wales. The king was personally involved in arranging the establishment of Flemish settlers in Dyfed. Native Welsh princes came under the king's direct influence, attending his courts. They gave hostages to the king as an indication rather than a guarantee of their client status and their future compliance. The assertion of royal power in Wales has long been acknowledged, but the greater emphasis placed upon it in recent studies is a major readjustment in our understanding of Wales in the twelfth century.

In Ireland, the position was subtly different. There had been hints that William I and William II might have an interest in Ireland, derived largely from the influence established by Archbishop Lanfranc, but the first real threat came with the accession of Henry II. The prospect of an invasion and conquest of Ireland was raised in 1155, probably by Theobald, archbishop of Canterbury, and was discussed in the king's immediate circle. One magnate, John, count of Eu, dated a charter 'at Winchester in the year in which a conquest of Ireland was discussed' (Flanagan, 1989). The archbishop, working through his clerk, John of Salisbury, secured approval for such a venture from Pope Adrian IV. But the Empress

Matilda argued against the idea, and the project was dropped. The text of Adrian's approval, preserved by Gerald of Wales, was couched in very general terms: it was 'pleasing and acceptable' that Henry should 'enter that island for the purpose of enlarging the boundaries of the church, checking the descent into wickedness, correcting morals and implanting virtues, and encouraging the faith of Christ', and that the people of that land should receive him honourably as their lord.

In the event, the initial invasion of Ireland in 1169 was a baronial enterprise, carried out with Henry's guarded approval. In 1171, when Earl Richard de Clare was recognized as King Dermot's successor in Leinster, Henry's attitude hardened and he made ready for a personal intervention in Ireland. Earl Richard returned to Wales and agreed to hold his Irish lands from the king, while Irish rulers made clear their acceptance of the prospect of Henry's direct intervention in their country. In October 1171 he landed at Waterford, to require the submission of Anglo-Norman and Irish leaders. The size of his army and the heavy equipment he brought to Ireland made clear that, if the threat of force was not effective, he would seek to win submission by battle, and Normans and Irish were quick to submit and to acknowledge his authority. Pope Alexander III endorsed his claims and his action. Henry had ensured that Ireland should not become a country where independent Anglo-Norman magnates could establish their power; it was not to be a replica of south and mid-Wales. The appointment of justiciars to keep the Anglo-Norman barons in check, the establishment of a royal base and royal administrators at Dublin, and ultimately the introduction of English law in the reign of Henry III, all flowed from Henry II's initial stance. The lawful nature of his claims over Ireland grew out of papal approval and the ready acceptance of Anglo-Norman and Irish leaders alike. In his survey of Henry II's reign, Lewis Warren (1973) presents the case in strong terms that, with Anglo-Norman mercenaries serving under an Irish dynasty in Leinster, Norman incursions into Ireland might have resembled the spread of Norman influence in Scotland. Richard de Clare did not see his opportunities in those terms. Unchecked, as heir and successor to King Dermot, he might have created in Ireland a pattern similar to that which the Guiscards created in Sicily. Such a possibility was prevented by Henry II's bold claims and firm action.

In all these theatres of warfare the Normans owed much to their technical skills and discipline as fighting men. Their use of cavalry, with mounted knights working as a unit, gave them an advantage over all the opponents they encountered in Britain. In the eleventh and early twelfth centuries the knight was not a man of high social standing; he was a trained fighter with expensive equipment. The javelin, whether thrown or couched, was a dangerous weapon. The weight of a cavalry charge was not easily withstood. When cavalry were used with archers in support the combination was often deadly, especially when (as happened in Ireland) the archers were themselves mounted. Regularly the skill and daring of individual leaders could swing the balance in favour of a Norman force outnumbered by their opponents. Success could depend upon such men as Roger of Beaumont at the battle of Hastings in 1066, Robert of Rhuddlan in north Wales in the 1070s and 1080s, or Raymond le Gros in Ireland in 1169–70.

In Anglo-Saxon England, the royal armies might use horses to travel at speed, but they fought on foot, armed with weapons intended for hand-to-hand fighting, the battle axe, the spear and the sword. In a defensive position, as at the battle of Hastings, they were hard to dislodge. In a surprise attack they could overwhelm an enemy, as Harold Godwinesson did at Rhuddlan and Stamford Bridge; in a mobile encounter, such as at Fulford Gate, victory would depend on numbers, superior skills and sheer survival. The core of the English armies comprised professional fighters, thegns or housecarls, who could claim an expertise in arms, whether through birth or through deliberate and constant training; but there was also something of a peasant army, drawn from the rural neighbourhood, whose arms, training and discipline left much to be desired.

Duke William had put his claim to England to the test of pitched battle near Hastings, where mobility and training prevailed. But his resources were tested to the limit in a different kind of warfare in 1069–70, when English insurgents were supported by a Danish fleet operating in the Humber estuary. The English used the terrain to good advantage and adopted a form of guerilla warfare enshrined in the career and legend of Hereward the Wake. To contain his enemies William needed to operate in depth with a series of base camps. If the Normans put the Danish fleet in danger the Danes need only move to the opposite bank of the Humber and the Normans had to extend their forces along both banks of the estuary. However, over a long and difficult campaign William's commanders adapted their tactics and wore down the opposition.

When King William's forces were matched against men trained and equipped for cavalry fighting he met with little success. His campaign in Brittany in 1076, intended to punish Ralph de Gael, resulted in failure, and the open battle between the Conqueror and his son, Robert Curthose, at Gerberoi in 1079, was another humiliating failure.

The response to successful attacks by the Normans varied. In England, the death of King Harold and his brothers at the battle of Hastings removed the country's natural leaders, and no other family produced an effective alternative. Divided counsels and rival ambitions among men of influence, and what appears to have been a collapse of morale among the military elite, destroyed any hope of sustained opposition to the Norman invaders. The potential may have been there, but the sources can only hint at that. At Gerberoi, the Conqueror owed his life to an Englishman. Toki, son of Wigot, of Wallingford, at the cost of his own life, found him a fresh horse and made it possible for him to continue the battle. When William Rufus became king in 1087 he was able to mobilize English loyalty and call up English forces in his efforts to defend himself against Duke Robert of Normandy, though the impact may have been political rather than military. In Wales early Norman advances were sporadic, and conquests were limited in range. In north Wales in the last two decades of the eleventh century, and in south Wales during much of the twelfth century, Norman resources could be stretched to the limit, and the invaders could not muster the forces necessary to ensure either large-scale or permanent victory.

On the other hand, Celtic leaders in Wales and Ireland could rarely find an effective answer to Norman superiority in the field.

The writer of the Welsh *Brut y Tywysogion* recorded with regret that a Norman force could retire, regroup and return to the attack, and that their attacks could be sustained for a long day's fighting, while Welsh resistance weakened steadily. In Wales, as in Ireland, a bold charge by a small troop of mounted men could leave a much larger force in total disarray. In that lay the secret of Raymond le Gros at Baginbun in 1169 and of John de Courcy in his invasion of Ulidia in 1177. In Ireland the Celtic kings could not match the Anglo-Norman technical superiority, and there – as in England a century earlier – the quality of leadership was fatally flawed. Rory O'Connor, nominally high king from 1166, was less than effective, often directing his forces against Irish enemies, with little realization of the long-term threat of Anglo-Norman settlement. The multiplicity of clans and septs, kings and kingdoms, gave the intruders the chance of piecemeal local conquests. Throughout these critical years Irish armies showed great courage but made little headway against Anglo-Norman commanders.

Castles were essential to Norman success and at times to their survival. In the earliest phases of conquest castles that depended upon earthworks were built, often at great speed. They continued to be in constant use in England and at various stages in Wales and Ireland, and they proved to be equally valuable in the Scottish kingdom. The classic types were the ringwork and the motte and bailey. A ringwork was essentially an enclosure defended by ditch and bank with a strongly fortified gatehouse, while the motte and bailey depended upon a mound, usually man-made, and a court-yard or bailey which would have earth embankments as its primary defence. Both motte and bailey could have a deep ditch and would be further strengthened by stout wooden palisades. In England, as in Normandy, there has been a tendency to underestimate the number of ringworks, partly because ringworks were frequently developed into mottes, and their original form can then only be established by excavation. The basic distinction between ringwork and motte and bailey may lead to grave oversimplification. Excavations at Penmaen in Wales and Castletobin in Ireland reveal ringworks of very similar pattern. Earthworks at Berkhamsted and Pleshey and early castles abandoned in favour of later, more sophisticated strongholds, such as Williams Hill at Middleham or Twthill at Rhuddlan, demonstrate the simple form of motte and bailey. The size of the mottes at Clare, Oxford and Thetford in England, Cardiff in Wales, and Urr in Scotland indicate clearly the formidable obstacle that such a castle could present. There were many variations. A number of castles, among them Arundel, Clun and Windsor, had more than one bailey; Lewes had two mottes, each covering an exposed quarter of the site.

In Normandy there was a tradition of strongly built stone castles in which the basic defence lay in a freestanding stone keep. The foundations of such a keep at Fécamp and the more substantial remains at Caen represent this type of castle. Almost impregnable against direct assault, such strongholds could hold out against everything except starvation and, less frequently, successful mining operations. The Conqueror and his sons built such castles in England: the Tower of London, Colchester and Rochester are the best examples, but they could be matched by many later keeps built by Henry I and Henry II and by a number of their magnates.

England had no tradition of castle-building before the Norman conquest. A small number had been built by Normans who settled in England in the reign of Edward the Confessor. Among these, Richard's Castle was established on the Shropshire border by Richard son of Scrob, and a similar motte and bailey was established at Hereford by the Confessor's nephew, Earl Ralph. Early reports on excavations at Goltho, in Lincolnshire, raised intriguing questions, suggesting an earthwork castle that antedated the conquest. Later interpretation indicated a moated site, used over a long period for domestic occupation, with a small motte built into the defences in the last decades of the eleventh century. William of Poitiers, writing in Normandy, was convinced that a castle existed at Dover and believed that there were other strongholds which Earl Harold might hold in the duke's interest while the Confessor was still alive. It is clear that there was no network of castles, nor any defensive line which the English might seek to hold in order to block a Norman advance. The Normans may, perhaps, have seen towns as fortified and defensible, and it has been suggested that Pevensey and Hastings were deliberately targeted in the autumn of

1066 because they were boroughs with rudimentary but effective defences.

In Wales and along the Welsh border many earthwork castles were established. The motte at Cardiff is the largest in south Wales, and on the Herefordshire border the Lacy castle at Ewyas Lacy (Longtown) still retains something of its forbidding appearance. Roger of Montgomery's castle at Hen Domen, Montgomery, has a deceptively simple and peaceful appearance which belies the threat it offered to mid-Wales in the eleventh and twelfth centuries. In the north, Robert of Rhuddlan's castles at Rhuddlan itself and at Degannwy were the twin bases from which much of Gwynedd was threatened and overrun. Roger de Pîtres and his family had a castle at Caldicot which belongs to the reign of the Conqueror; it was then a subsidiary stronghold in the castlery of Chepstow. Brecon castle, established by Bernard of Neufmarché early in the 1090s, was intended as, and remained, the principal castle of his new lordship.

Two castles of great significance for Wales relied from the beginning on stone defences. At Ludlow the curtain walling has been dated to the late eleventh century. At Chepstow a stone keep was built on the Welsh side of the Wye. The work was started before 1071, and the castlery was to be a major area of Norman activity throughout and beyond the Conqueror's reign. The keep was a two-storey hall with a bailey running along the cliff where the land sloped down towards the river level. Continuous expansion and rebuilding could not disguise the original plan of the castle.

Ireland presents a particularly intriguing problem. For many decades before the arrival of the Normans, Irish kings made use of heavily fortified enclosures, a rath, a dún or a ringwork. Some of these older fortified sites were being abandoned by the early years of the twelfth century. Before 1086, Turlough O'Brien ceased to rely on the defences of his fortress at Kincora and began to develop Limerick as a capital. In 1101, Murchetach O'Brien gave the rock of Cashel of the kings to the church, and in the same year he found the northern stronghold of Aileach undefended when he attacked and demolished it. When, in the early stages of his long career, Tiernan O'Rourke became lord of Bréifne in 1125, he had his chief fort at Drumahair, and that appears to be a continuation of the older tradition.

During the twelfth century, in a small number of cases, a stronghold was being described as a *caislen*, a castle. Turlough O'Connor built a castle at Athlone in 1129 specifically to defend the bridge across the Shannon. It was one of three castles ascribed to him and given this new name. Turlough had married a daughter to Arnulf of Montgomery, lord of Pembroke, one of the powerful family of Bellême, and when Henry I drove that family out of England in 1102 Arnulf took refuge in Ireland, with his wife's kin. Norman influence could easily lie behind Turlough's use of castles, strategically sited, and built specifically for defence purposes. Athlone had a chequered history. Before 1135, it had been destroyed and rebuilt twice and it survived until it was demolished again in 1155. After a long hiatus, it was replaced by a motte and bailey some time before 1199, a castle established to guard the river crossing, and John de Grey was responsible for building a powerful stone castle there early in the thirteenth century. Further west, in Galway, Rory O'Connor built a castle at Tuam as a new base for his authority in Connacht. In the same decade, in Leinster, Dermot Mac Murrough was said to have a castle at Ferns. These, with two other fortifications at Ballinasloe and Collooney, were identified as *caislen*. With the exception of Ferns, none of these castles have survived, and it is impossible to say whether they represent a new type of fortification or a new attitude towards the use of fortified sites. At Ferns, excavation suggests that a ringwork with a fortified entry was constructed on the site now dominated by the ruins of the Marshal castle, but whether it was built by Dermot or Richard fitz Gilbert (Strongbow) cannot be established.

A single stronghold might dominate an area and be the key to survival, but the strength of many lordships depended upon a network of castles. The Lacy family, with frontier lands in Herefordshire and southern Shropshire, and later with extensive holdings in Ireland, were under constant pressure to provide adequate defences. Surviving remains of castles and castle sites demonstrate the scale, though not perhaps the full scope, of their operations. In Herefordshire, with major strongholds at Weobley,

Ewyas Lacy (Longtown), Ewyas Harold and Castle Frome, they had castles on demesne estates at Cusop, Bacton, Lyde, Yarkhill, Stoke Lacy and Leominster, and on an estate they held as sub-tenants at Almeley. The area they controlled in Shropshire was centred on their manor of Stanton Lacy, in which Ludlow castle was founded. Their tenants had castles at Middlehope, Rushbury, Corfton, Hopton Wafers, Stokesay and perhaps Plaish. The most striking survival of these lesser castles is the splendid motte, with sections of the moat and of the defences of the bailey still undisturbed, at Holdgate (Stanton Long). Despite changes in tenure, especially in Shropshire, the family had long experience of castle-building and of defence in depth. When, in 1171–2, Hugh de Lacy acquired Meath, he could call upon a tradition of frontier defence extending back to the earliest years of the Norman occupation of England. It is no surprise to find that the site of one of his principal castles at Drogheda should still be dominated by a well-preserved motte and that his chief castle at Trim should be encircled by a ring of lordships and castles, from Granard, Mullingar, Delvin and Rathwire in the west to Galtrim and Skreen in the east.

Apart from their wider strategic value, castles were protection for the estates and the people from which the lord or his castellan drew his resources. That raises the question: how do we explain the nature of settlement and the relationship between the settlers and the indigenous population? It can be and has for long been answered in terms of lordship. The influential settlers, the men of power, were drawn from different levels of the aristocracy or from that group which was growing steadily in stature in the twelfth century, the knights. The exploitation of estates for their maintenance and benefit was a common feature in western Europe. In England a wealth of documentation enables us to speak with precision about rights of lordship. Charters in which rights of lordship were transferred, whether to lay tenants or to the church, financial records, and a multiplicity of legal records, all contribute to our knowledge. If we use terms appropriate to lordship, we are using and seeking to understand the language of documents produced by Anglo-Norman landowners. In the large majority of cases the barons had to deal with scattered estates. From the early years of the conquest a small number of magnates, already powerful in Normandy, acquired rich lordships in England. The lesser magnates and their principal tenants held estates spread over a number of shires. Their charters often demonstrate the means by which a substantial honor could be administered. The principal castle – the *caput honoris* – provided a focus for their activities. This helped to compensate for the problem of being an absentee landlord, if only in outlying manors.

Norman settlement in Wales presents the variation in the pattern of lordship in sharper terms. The family of Bellême had wide interests in France and England and violent change of fortune in one country affected the family elsewhere. Hugh of Avranches held Chester and controlled much of north Wales. But while he was involved at the king's court and in his Norman and English estates, his cousin, Robert of Rhuddlan, concentrated on his conquests in north Wales. The richest of Bernard of Neufmarché's lands lay in his lordship of Brecknock, while the Braose family was concerned with the Norman lordship of Briouze, the English honor of Bramber and, however marginally, their Welsh territory in Buellt. They spent more time in Wales after they had acquired the lordship of Brecknock in 1165, at least until King John's crony, William de Braose, embarked on his ambitious policy of seeking new wealth at the royal court and in Ireland. He was disgraced in 1207; he died in exile in 1211. After a further seven years in disfavour, the family was restored in 1218 but Bramber and Brecknock then passed to different branches of the family.

Even magnates holding exceptionally large honors exercised a wide degree of control and were familiar with much of their lordships. Barons did not habitually give their charters a place-date and the detailed itinerary of a twelfth-century baron cannot be established. Occasional indications of his whereabouts in charters and other contemporary sources may offer a limited guide to his movements. The earls of Gloucester held lands in many English shires and in south Wales, and they were familiar figures in many parts of their possessions. Earl Robert and his son Earl William used their residences at Cranborne and Tewkesbury and their castles at Bristol and Cardiff, and they occasionally noted that a charter had been issued at one of these familiar places. When Prince John acquired the earldom of Gloucester by marrying one of Earl William's daughters he, too, used these family possessions and issued charters while he was in residence. The lords of Richmond remained active as lords of a substantial fief in Brittany and Earl Conan became duke of Brittany in 1156. When they were in the duchy, they were not divorced from their English lordship; officials and tenants from the honor of Richmond travelled with them to France, and from Brittany they issued charters relating to their English honor. In England they issued charters from religious houses that enjoyed their patronage, St Mary's, York, and the abbey of St Edmund at Bury, from Boston, a town that grew under their protection, and from their castle at Richmond and their manor houses at Washingborough and Cheshunt. Domesday Book and the Pipe Rolls provide a great deal of information about the value of fiefs. From Domesday Book relative values for the Conqueror's reign can be established, and the Pipe Rolls often provide valuable information on occasions when a fief has passed into the king's hands. The earldom of Gloucester, to cite only one instance, was producing revenues of £580 when Earl William died in 1182. Moving further afield to Wales and Ireland, such precision is rarely possible. The accounts drawn up at Dublin for 1211–12 (the Irish Pipe Roll) include many details of the resources available in crops and livestock, as well as castles and boroughs, in the Lacy lordships of Meath and Ulster, which King John had taken into his own possession.

To explain the nature of settlement and the relationship between settlers and the local population in terms of lordship in the eleventh and twelfth centuries has been the method adopted by many medievalists. It was a theme finely tuned and used with subtlety by Sir Frank Stenton (1932). It lies behind much of David Douglas's reconstruction of Anglo-Norman society (1964, 1969, 1976) though he was concerned – perhaps obsessed – by notions of the Norman world that verged on pan-Normanism. It runs through the work of Frank Barlow (1955–1983); Kapelle (1979) could discuss Norman infiltration into northern England within this convention, and it is implicit in Marjorie Chibnall's *Anglo-Norman England* (1986).

In 1969 John Le Patourel, one of the most perceptive writers on Anglo-Norman history, produced a paper titled 'The Norman Colonization of Britain', the substance of which was incorporated into his book, *The Norman Empire* (1976). He saw in the Norman conquest of England a military phase followed by a colonizing phase, and his main thesis was that 'conquest and plunder were followed by colonization and exploitation'. He was much influenced by Lucien Musset's studies of the aristocracy of eleventh-century Normandy, and he argued for an aristocratic colonization of England, with Norman magnates and their principal tenants taking over the greater part of English landed estates. He saw also the large-scale benefactions which the Normans made to religious houses in Normandy, with the conquered land being milked for the benefit of the conquerors' homeland. Despite the limited nature of the evidence, he believed that Norman merchants also derived great wealth from the conquest. The coverage of towns in Domesday Book is erratic, but the record shows immigrants acquiring a share – perhaps a large share – in the trade of seven English boroughs, Cambridge, Hereford, Norwich, Shrewsbury, Southampton, Wallingford and York. London and Winchester were not covered in the survey, but later evidence shows Normans to be well established in both centres. He was convinced that this colonization was 'essentially aristocratic, ecclesiastic and mercantile' and that it was an ongoing process.

A colonial analogy may be very illuminating, but it needs careful qualification. Le Patourel was arguing for much more than an analogy. By comparison with later writers he examined a very restricted period, for he was concerned only with the Norman empire, which he considered to have come to an end with the conquest of Normandy by Geoffrey, count of Anjou, in 1144. He was fully aware of a limited definition of 'colonization' within which his claims could be sustained.

For Wales and Ireland these issues have been presented in sharper terms. In 1974, Rees Davies published a seminal essay on

'Colonial Wales', and extensively developed this theme in his *Conquest, Coexistence, and Change* (1987) and *Domination and Conquest* (1990). French magnates are the crucial figures but the hard grind of settlement and colonization fell largely to their knights and tenants, with the subjugation of the local population and the settlement in a number of lordships of a rural working force recruited from outside Wales. Flemish settlers in Dyfed and Ceredigion were valuable pioneer farmers, while English settlers were much despised in Ceredigion. Towns, smaller and less prosperous than English boroughs, were important centres of foreign influence. The Normans were prodigal in their grants of Welsh lands and churches to monastic houses in France and England.

For a popular survey of the Anglo-Norman period in Ireland, Robin Frame used the title *Colonial Ireland* (1981). His principal theme was that, with Anglo-Norman settlements, Ireland experienced something more than a superficial and incomplete military conquest and suffered a deeper colonization. One feature that stands out in contrast to England and Wales is the extent to which an alien working population was imported into the country. Magnates acquiring land in Ireland brought English, Welsh and Flemish peasants to work the soil, and in Ulster there was the additional implantation of migrants from Scotland. Both Davies and Frame emphasize the fact that the recognition of this colonial pattern depends upon a long view. They approach an earlier age of conquest from studies of a later period, Davies in his impressive *Lordship and Society in the March of Wales 1282–1400* (1978a), and Frame in his *English Lordship in Ireland 1318–1361* (1982). The period extends from the early years of invasion and conquest to the end of the thirteenth century, with some evidence adduced, or analogies drawn, from the reign of Edward I. Certainly, the extent to which English magnates in the early fourteenth century were exploiting their Welsh lordships suggests a greatly increased scale of demands: large gifts of money, heavy renders in kind and the extension, or more accurately abuse, of rights of jurisdiction are all characteristic of the administration of Welsh lordships in the later middle ages. Davies identifies the process as an intensification of lordship, and it is a factor not to be ignored.

Social and administrative changes were accompanied by strong racial antipathies and often indeed by open hatred. In his *Gerald of Wales, 1146–1223*, Robert Bartlett (1982) explored the extent to which writers in western Europe in the eleventh and twelfth centuries used the convention of writing of races living on the fringes of their societies as 'barbarians'. Here, the greater precision of norms of marriage and inheritance in 'civilized' societies, formulated in the work of clerical reformers and writers, was an important influence. The glaring deficiencies, as they came to be identified, of England's Celtic neighbours recur in the works of a number of twelfth-century historians. The works of Gerald of Wales, especially those on Ireland, were central to Bartlett's theme. In *The Making of Europe* (1993) Bartlett has extended the range of his studies, and it is possible to see these racial issues in Britain in a wider context, as well as to examine the extent to which conquest, subjugation and colonization are interrelated.

For Scotland, the concept of colonization must be changed; what has served elsewhere in Britain will not stand. Geoffrey Barrow (1980) is fully committed to the view that there was a large-scale process of colonization. An Anglo-Norman aristocracy was introduced into and endowed in Scotland, and Le Patourel's 'aristocratic colonization' can be identified. At a lower level of society there was substantial Flemish and English settlement and the planting of alien communities to exploit the country's natural resources is plain to see. But we shall find no conquest and no exploitation for the benefit of a foreign homeland; antipathy between native Scottish and Anglo-Norman settlers there was, but the racial hatred which marked Wales and Ireland is not a dominant characteristic. Changes in the Scottish church were sponsored and encouraged by the monarchy; new men and new ideas were welcomed into the kingdom, but only a few houses in England derived any benefit from possessions in Scotland. Whatever concept of colonization we may use, it is different in scope from the language used by Welsh and Irish historians. It is a healthy warning not to allow a single concept to play too great a part in interpreting the past.

2

The Conquest of England

The Norman conquest and settlement in England evolved gradually. In the aftermath of the battle of Hastings, at a time when incisive leadership was vital, the English faced a crisis. Within fifteen days, four brothers of the house of Godwine had been killed and their sister Edith was distraught with grief; a successor who could rally support and coordinate immediate action against the Normans was essential.

Despite his lack of experience, Edgar the Atheling emerged as the obvious successor to the throne, though support was limited and less than enthusiastic. The northern earls, Edwin and Morcar, drew back to await events. The Normans took Dover and moved on to receive the submission of Canterbury, where they were forced to remain for more than three weeks, made vulnerable by widespread illness. No attack came, and the opportunity of effective hostilities was lost. Local communities in the south-east began to submit, and William was able to resume the offensive and to move in a wide arc on a slow progress to London. There the prospect of a firm defence evaporated and English leaders left the city for Berkhamsted where they submitted to William. He was crowned king on Christmas Day 1066 at Westminster Abbey. The Norman hold on London was precarious and Norman troops were nervous: shouts of acclamation in the abbey roused fears that fighting had broken out and the troops began to set fire to neighbouring buildings. Order was

Map 1   England: principal places mentioned in the text

restored, the coronation rites were completed and Edward the Confessor's preferred successor was the lawful king.

For the first five years of his reign, William the Conqueror had two major issues to resolve. Could he contain sporadic outbreaks of opposition and revolt and impose his authority over the whole kingdom? Could he weld together Norman and English elements in his court, in the church, and in his administration? From 1067 until 1070 he was faced by a series of local challenges, at Exeter, in Dover, in the midlands and along the western frontier of England and Wales and in East Anglia. Each outbreak was, from an English point of view, a refusal to accept Norman rule, and from a Norman point of view, a rebellion against a lawful king. Vigorous campaigning, under William's leadership, and sorties by small garrisons which were bold to the point of being reckless gave the Normans the advantage until 1069. Their hold on the south-east was secure; the basis for a firm control in south-western England had been established; the midlands were partially subdued; and the first steps had been taken to stabilize and hold the frontier between England and Wales. Beyond the Humber Norman power rested on outposts, uneasily held; York was a danger point, strategically too important to neglect, and was defended by two castles, while the far north was hostile territory still to be subdued, with Durham a remote and dangerous base.

The north provided the sternest test of Norman strength. In Northumbria, government through local magnates proved a failure, and William's first attempt to impose a Norman administrator ended in disaster. Robert de Commines was sent to Durham with a strong contingent and he was warned that an English force was active in the area. Whether through over-confidence or failure to treat the intelligence seriously, he billeted his troops in Durham and took no precautions against attack. Overnight, the city was surrounded and Robert and his men were slaughtered. Early in 1069 violence erupted at York, and the city had to be retaken and subdued. Elsewhere there was dangerous unrest. Eadric the Wild was active, chiefly on the western borders of the old earldom of Mercia, where Chester and Shrewsbury were under threat, though the rising affected an area extending as far east as Stafford.

In the summer of 1069 a large Danish fleet despatched by Swein Estrithson landed in the Humber, and this was a signal for English dissidents under Edgar the Atheling, Earl Waltheof and Cospatric of Northumbria to join them. York was their first target, but once the city had fallen the Scandinavian leaders showed a strange lack of purpose or policy. They fortified Axeholme as a base and mingled freely with the farmers of Lindsey, themselves of Danish stock. In due course they settled there for the winter. The Normans had to adopt an unfamiliar strategy, penetrating a difficult area in depth and maintaining a close watch on the invaders. That the Danish leaders did not put William under immediate pressure was ominous for the king's English opponents. Winter was at hand, but he was able to strike across to Stafford to take the first steps to check Eadric. Instead of returning to Lindsey, as he had intended, he turned towards York, which was once again in Danish hands. As he approached the city he laid waste a swathe of territory along his route. In the first months of the new year he set out deliberately to destroy all means of livelihood throughout Yorkshire and the neighbouring countryside, inflicting heavy losses and creating the conditions for starvation and famine. The savagery seems to have persuaded the Danish leaders to make terms, on condition that they could winter on the northern bank of the Humber. In a complex and difficult campaign William struck north and received the submission of the two northern magnates, Waltheof and Cospatric. Then he swung west across the Pennines to deal with the threat to Chester and Shrewsbury before he once more turned his attention to Lincolnshire. The Danes still represented a problem which he could not easily solve. Early in 1070, King Swein joined them; some of his men were linked with Hereward the Wake in his attack on Peterborough Abbey. The Danes were not to be put down by force; they were removed by negotiation and, as in 1069, William clearly made concessions to secure their departure.

Two aspects of this episode are particularly worthy of note. The first is the adaptability of the Normans on campaign. Here was no open victory for an elite cavalry force. The use of defence in depth, endurance and hard travel, which was said to have driven William's army close to mutiny – these were the hallmarks of the campaign.

The second aspect is the unbridled savagery of the Conqueror's policy. It reflected a streak of savagery in the king himself, which was rarely given expression, perhaps in the harrying of Harold's estates in the weeks before the battle of Hastings, and certainly in the deliberate laying waste of land around London later in 1066. Writing more than sixty years after the event, Orderic Vitalis was forthright in his condemnation of a crime against humanity. Perhaps a military historian might also see it as a sign of the ruthlessness which the Normans were never afraid to use on critical, if rare, occasions.

The military problem may have been resolved by 1171, but the political problem, so closely associated with it, was intractable. Could William (to restate the question) weld together Norman and English elements in his court, in the church and in his administration? The clearest pointer to his intentions was that a number of writs were issued in Latin and Anglo-Saxon and, on rare occasions, in Anglo-Saxon alone. In the early years of his reign he envisaged a society in which Englishmen of wealth and power would acknowledge him and work with him. It was not an impossible ambition. When the Conqueror marched against Exeter in 1067 he had English soldiers in his army. When illegitimate sons of King Harold raided in the Bristol Channel they were repulsed by the citizens of Bristol, and when they attempted a landing in Somerset Eadnoth the Staller (a general term to describe a royal attendant) led the thegns of the shire against them; he died in the encounter. Among the churchmen who served him, Aldred, archbishop of York, was loyal until his death in 1069, and Wulfstan, bishop of Worcester, was a valuable supporter both for William I and for William Rufus. English bishops appeared at the royal court until 1070, when Stigand, archbishop of Canterbury, and a number of his fellow-bishops were removed and replaced by men drawn from the continent. English abbots were replaced more slowly and appeared often as witnesses to the king's charters.

What of the greater nobles? The sources identify as especially significant figures, Edgar the Atheling, Earl Edwin and Earl Morcar, and Waltheof, son of Earl Siward, who had been given an earldom by the Confessor very late in his reign. To win Waltheof's loyalty, William gave him a niece, Judith, in marriage. There was talk of giving Edwin one of his own daughters as a wife, but the scheme was never carried out, perhaps because William's Norman barons would not accept an arrangement that would keep another large body of estates intact and severely limit their chances of making gains in the midlands. These were the natural leaders of the English; the Anglo-Saxon Chronicle suggests that there were 'other good men' with them, but none are named. Edgar was taken as a hostage to Normandy in 1067, and he found refuge in Scotland the following year. His greatest influence would be exercised at a later stage; for the present, he was the pretender who might prove dangerous.

At times the three earls attended William's court and attested his charters. The king addressed writs to Edwin and Waltheof assuming their cooperation. But there were times when revolt seemed their best response to the new regime. Edwin and Morcar joined Edgar in 1068 and had later to make their peace. Waltheof and Cospatric of Northumbria joined Edgar in 1069 and were forced into submission during the Conqueror's successful northern campaign. Their chances of victory in that year may have been much reduced because Edwin and Morcar remained loyal. In 1071, too late to be of value, they became implicated in Hereward the Wake's continued resistance; Morcar was captured in East Anglia and died in prison; Edwin remained at large but was murdered by his own men while travelling to Scotland. Waltheof survived until 1075, when he was drawn into the rebellion of Roger, earl of Hereford, and Ralph, earl of Norfolk. That was put down by the king's agents; it was notable that Wulfstan of Worcester and Aethelwig of Evesham joined forces with Walter de Lacy and Urse d'Abetot to oppose the earl of Hereford, who submitted and was condemned to long imprisonment. Earl Ralph escaped to Brittany; Waltheof was imprisoned and in 1076 he was executed. He was the last English magnate of the first rank to survive as a prominent figure in national politics. Others continued to serve the Conqueror, but they were men of lesser standing. William's charters show that in the early years of the reign he was able to rely on English administrators. Writs were addressed to Eadnoth and Bundi, the Stallers, and to English sheriffs, among them Tofi of Somerset, Edmund of Hertfordshire, Swawold of Oxford and Gosfrith the portreeve of London.

A striking feature about these men of high profile was that their power was not passed on to a new generation. Sheriffs were replaced by Frenchmen, such as Roger de Pîtres, Urse d'Abetot, Robert d'Oilli and Geoffrey de Mandeville, whose kindred continued to hold office after their death. Waltheof's estates and earldom passed through his daughter to the family of St Liz and, later, to David I of Scotland. Cospatric of Northumbria found refuge in Scotland and received a landed endowment, which passed to his heirs as lords of Dunbar. His fellow exile Marleswein founded a family in Scotland, which was prominent in the twelfth century.

Some old English families survived as modest landholders. Alfsi of Faringdon, a powerful local magnate in the Confessor's reign, left a son whose descendents were still established in Oxfordshire in the twelfth century. In Lincolnshire, the heirs of a certain Colgrim survived: his grandson, Alexander of Ingoldsby, was a substantial landholder, and in the next generation Nigel of Ingoldsby was sheriff of Lincolnshire. At Bristol a local dynasty survived and acquired wealth and power: Eadnoth the Staller and his son Harding carried the family over the critical years of the conquest, and Harding's son Robert was a wealthy citizen and a close ally of the young prince, Henry fitz Empress. When Henry became king he was given the rich lordship of Berkeley. Marriage with the daughter of an English family could produce a Norman dynasty with English blood. The wife of Geoffrey de la Guerche (whose lands later formed part of the Mowbray honor) was a certain Aelfgeofu. Robert d'Oilli held lands in Oxfordshire once held by Wigot of Wallingford, probably acquired by marriage to Wigot's daughter. A small number of families, especially in Northumbria, could claim continuity from pre-conquest England. But the record, taken as a whole, is meagre.

The sad fate for the generality of Old-English thegns must be found elsewhere. Many died in battle, and their lands were forfeit. King William issued a writ to Baldwin, abbot of Bury St Edmunds, ordering him to hand over the land of those of his men who had fought against the king and died at the battle of Hastings; for their families the future was bleak. Domesday Book provides evidence in abundance that men of substance were reduced to holding as tenants of Norman lords parts of what had once been their own estates. For many it was survival at a bitter price. Others found their escape in exile, some in Scandinavia, others as far afield as Byzantium.

The distribution of the spoils among the victorious Frenchmen was complex and extended over a number of years. Lands declared forfeit in the immediate aftermath of the battle of Hastings might be easy to claim where the Normans already had control, but the grant of estates held by one named Anglo-Saxon landowner created title to land in areas yet to be subdued. Revolts against King William added to the body of lands available for distribution. Estates held by Marleswein, sheriff of Lincolnshire, were at the king's disposal after 1068, Earl Morcar's lands in 1070, and Earl Edwin's in 1071. Edwin's estates were handed over to a number of beneficiaries; in Warwickshire (to cite only one county) they included the count of Meulan, Ralph de Limésy and William fitz Ansculf, as well as Christina, sister of Edgar the Atheling, and Thorkell of Warwick. His Yorkshire estates passed eventually to Count Alan the Red of Brittany, to form his castlery and lordship of Richmond. With Waltheof's fall from grace and execution in 1076, the greater part of his lands was retained by his widow, the Countess Judith, but many of his estates, especially land held by his men, came into the hands of the king to be retained or distributed to new tenants. Roger of Bully had a large holding in England; it included estates formerly held by Morcar, Edwin and Waltheof. He reaped the benefit of continuous royal generosity. That the transfer of land was sometimes a subtle process can be seen in the Domesday entry for Edwin's manor of Bloxham, which recorded that from Earl Tostig's time Saegeat, a thegn, had lived there, once as a free man: Earl Edwin gave him to Ralph d'Oilli, who restored him to the king's lordship.

The king retained in his own hands about 20 per cent of the resources of his new kingdom, some of which was committed to the support of Edward the Confessor's widow and minor royal officials. William acquired manors in most of the English shires, including seven in which the Confessor had not held any land. Only in Sussex, Herefordshire, Shropshire and Cheshire were exceptional arrangements made: the king's control of royal estates in Herefordshire was restored after the death of William fitz Osbern in 1071, and conditions in Shropshire changed radically when Henry I destroyed the power of Robert of Bellême. In some shires the Domesday record points to a distinction between royal estates formerly held by the Confessor and estates acquired during the course of William's reign. The king's half-brothers, Odo, bishop of Bayeux, and Robert, count of Mortain, had large fiefs which brought another 7 per cent under the direct control of the new dynasty, though a more accurate analysis emerges if their lands are included among those of the greater lordships of the realm. Then we can say that eleven magnates had lands which yielded more than about £750 a year. They included two independent lords – Eustace, count of Boulogne, and Count Alan the Red, a member of the cadet branch of the ducal family in Brittany. Two Norman lords were powerful kinsmen of the Conqueror, William fitz Osbern and, more remotely, Roger of Montgomery. Hugh of Avranches, vicomte of the Avranchin, and Richard fitz Gilbert were drawn from well-established Norman families. Geoffrey, bishop of Coutances, and William de Warenne were men of modest wealth in Normandy who were greatly enriched in England. Geoffrey de Mandeville's standing and wealth in the duchy cannot be established.

Closely linked with this group of well-endowed magnates are Robert, count of Eu, and his son William, whose combined estates in England yielded £690 a year. They, too, were kinsmen of the king. In financial terms, this small group of men enjoyed 20 per cent of England's wealth. Some of them had invested heavily in the enterprise of England, providing large numbers of ships for the invasion fleet. Robert, count of Mortain, was credited with 120 ships, Bishop Odo with 100, and Hugh of Avranches, Robert, count of Eu, Roger of Montgomery and William fitz Osbern were each credited with sixty. Their rewards may be said to reflect their contributions to victory though others, who were credited with having provided a substantial number of ships, did not fare so well (Hollister, 1987).

Although there were about 180 immigrant lords holding lands in chief of the crown, the greater share of these lands was granted to a small group of less than fifty magnates; they held, in terms of value, some 37 per cent of the kingdom. Assessing the wealth and influence of those who were richly endowed but not among the richest tenants-in-chief cannot be judged by one criterion alone. Robert Malet held the honor of Eye and served the Conqueror as chamberlain. Hugh of Montfort was the king's constable. They and other curial officers reaped the benefit of constant attendance upon the king; the difference in their wealth was less significant than a statistical comparison might suggest. Ralph of Tosny was well endowed in his own right, and with the holding of his brother Robert of Stafford, the family was greatly enriched in England. Henry of Ferrers held land in many shires but he owed much of his strength to the concentration of lands in his castlery of Tutbury. So, too, on a smaller scale did Hugh de Port, sheriff of Hampshire, who held manors as tenant-in-chief worth £250 a year, many of them in his own shire. As tenant of Odo, bishop of Bayeux, he had estates valued at £47, and when Odo was imprisoned these may have been regarded as tenure *in capite*. But elsewhere Hugh also held lands as a mesne tenant worth £170 a year. To judge his standing and wealth, with some £470 a year, he must be compared with magnates of great status. Such examples could be produced from many parts of the country.

Within the greater lordships, as magnates gave estates to knights in their service, some of the mesne tenants acquired substantial holdings and were barons of their honors. In Count Alan's lord-ship of Richmond those who were his leading tenants in the Conqueror's reign were the ancestors of influential and compara-tively wealthy families: the hereditary stewards who later took the name of Thornton and the lords of Middleham, each holding fifteen fees, the hereditary constables with thirteen fees and cham-berlains with eleven fees, the Musters and the Furneaux each with eight fees, the Valognes and the de la Mares each with seven fees, the Lascelles and Mumbys each with five fees. Another holding of five fees came to be identified by the name of a twelfth-century tenant, Conan, son of Ellis. These were powerful dynasties in Lincolnshire and Yorkshire.

Changes in tenure, confusion over title to land and unlawful intrusion created many problems. The king was determined that the whole process should be conducted lawfully. A number of land pleas settled major conflicts of interest: the monks of Ely had to vindicate their claims; at Pinnenden Heath disputes between Lanfranc, archbishop of Canterbury, and Odo, bishop of Bayeux (acting as earl of Kent), were investigated; the abbey of Fécamp and William de Braose brought their conflict of interest in Sussex to trial. Duplicate entries in Domesday Book and, occasionally, brief accounts of the descent of a manor over the years of settlement point to less significant conflicts. Lists of disputes (*clamores*) for Huntingdon, Lincolnshire and Yorkshire give details of unlawful possession, quarrels over lordship and confused land transactions. One entry for the borough of Huntingdon records six changes of tenure for a parish church and its lands where the text of Domesday Book gives no hint of hidden problems. For the south-western counties of Somerset, Devon and Cornwall lists of appropriated lands (*terrae occupatae*), bound up with the manuscript of Exon Domesday, provide a range of additional information including disputed claims to land.

Many of the fiefs established by the Conqueror survived for generations, some for centuries; they were valuable for administrative and financial purposes long after their military importance had declined. The Clares built steadily on the basis of their Domesday possessions and became powerful in England, Wales and Ireland. Ralph Paynel succeeded to lands held by Marleswein and one branch of his descendants was firmly and widely based down to the fourteenth century. Richmond remained with Count Alan's direct male heirs, who succeeded to the duchy of Brittany in 1156. In the next generation it passed to an heiress, Constance, wife of Henry II's son Geoffrey; the murder of their son Arthur meant that once again the inheritance passed through the female line. The lordship was still an entity throughout the later middle ages. The honor of Warenne passed to a collateral line in 1119, Chester in 1120 and again in 1237. The heirs of Simon of St Liz and David I of Scotland held lands and titles derived from Earl Waltheof's earldom, the St Liz family surviving until 1184, the connection of the Scottish royal house until 1237. The smaller lordship of the Domesday tenant Guy de Craon remained in the direct line of succession until 1197. This small cross-section could be matched by many similar examples. Stability well into the twelfth century and, less often, into later periods is one factor of the Norman settlement which cannot be ignored.

On the other hand there were changes. Death, forfeiture and the king's desire to use and reward new men were the obvious causes. Geoffrey de la Guerche died early in the reign of William Rufus and the king used his estates as part of the fief he set up for Robert of Stuteville, who fell foul of Henry I and forfeited his lordship in 1106. William II created new lordships elsewhere, especially to strengthen the defences of northern England, with castles and baronies established at Skipton, Barnard Castle and Carlisle. In the secure areas of southern and eastern England Henry I established new baronies at Kington and Bourne. Pre-eminently, he created the honor and earldom of Gloucester for one of the ablest of his illegitimate sons, Robert. Henry also built up the defences of the north in a systematic way, using men he could trust and establishing new castles and lordships. Soon after Robert of Stuteville's estates were declared forfeit in 1106 they were used as the basis for a new honor for one of the king's able young men from Normandy, Nigel d'Aubigny, who became a leading magnate in Northumberland. Two experienced administrators were established: Eustace fitz John in the recently escheated honor of Tickhill and at the new castle at Alnwick, and Walter d'Espec at Helmsley and Wark-on-Tweed. A string of new fortifications and lesser lordships in Northumberland, and especially in the Tyne and Tweed valleys, were the product of a deliberate and vigorous policy. The fluid element in Anglo-Norman society could be exploited to great advantage.

The control of land transactions by law and the distribution of land by the king's will demonstrate the basic principle of land tenure in Norman England. Land was the king's to be held of the king. In return it was burdened with duties. Domesday Book bears eloquent witness to the range of dues and renders that the king could claim from royal estates, but we must turn elsewhere for the range of dues he could claim from his tenants-in-chief. Their primary responsibility was to provide him with an efficient army: their honors carried a burden of knight service, their *servitium debitum*. The wealth they drew from their possessions made possible the provision of armed and trained knights. It was a system with which most of them were already familiar in Normandy, but the scale of their obligations was much greater in England.

The days have long gone when historians debated as a thorny question the introduction of knight service in England, with its concept of land held in return for military service. Links between land and service in pre-conquest England are now taken for granted in a way that was considered daring if not heretical less than fifty years ago. That a fiscal unit of five hides was capable of maintaining an armed fighting man – though not one trained to fight on horseback – is clear. That there was a military elite, earls, thegns and housecarls (household troops) is unquestionable. That the estates of Worcester Cathedral Priory, Tavistock and other ecclesiastical foundations were organized to produce a quota of fighting men capable of operating on sea or land has long since been established. With the Norman conquest a new element was added: the fighting man must be armed, equipped and trained to be part of a mounted army on the continental pattern. There had been some experiment before 1066 in training English troops to use the new techniques. The Confessor's nephew Ralph, earl of Hereford, used mounted soldiers in his attempts to defend the southern frontier between England and Wales, but they were inadequately trained for the crisis that faced them in 1055. After the conquest it was thought wiser to entrust land and resources to French lords and to recruit knights from across the Channel rather than to rely heavily on a native elite.

Before 1072 King William's tenants-in-chief had been burdened with their military obligations. The simplest method for producing a quota of knights was for their lord to clothe and house them himself; they were household knights. Later – perhaps not very much later – they could be given land on which to maintain themselves. At Abingdon the tradition was preserved that William I ordered the abbey to provide knights for castle-guard at Windsor and made it clear that knights who had come to England were the most suitable men for such duties. So Abbot Athelhelm employed mercenaries to meet the king's demand; enfeoffment came later. Apart from a few rare exceptions, the scale of the magnates' obligations can only be recovered from later evidence. In or before 1072, Abbot Aethelwig was ordered to bring to the king, fully equipped, the five knights he owed for Evesham Abbey's estates. Athelhelm was said to have enfeoffed thirty-one knights at Abingdon before 1083. Between 1093 and 1096 a list of the knights of the archbishopric of Canterbury was drawn up: sixty-six men held between them $98\frac{1}{4}$ fees. Abbot Baldwin of Bury St Edmunds drew up a 'feudal book': it cannot be dated precisely but it was compiled between 1087 and 1098. At Bury, thirty-six knights had been enfeoffed with land.

For the full range of knight service the critical documents are the barons' charters (*Cartae baronum*), issued in response to an enquiry by Henry II in 1166, and the detailed financial records in the Pipe Rolls. In 1166 Henry II wanted to know three things in detail: how many knights a tenant-in-chief had 'of old enfeoffment' before the death of Henry I in 1135; how many knights he had 'of new enfeoffment' since that date; how many knights were living in the household. The barons' replies give a detailed (though not complete) record of fees and of the men who held them. The highest quotas for the great ecclesiastical tenants were sixty for Canterbury, Winchester, Lincoln and Peterborough. For secular honors created by the Conqueror, among the highest quotas were eighty for Ferrers and seventy-five for Totnes; those expected to produce sixty knights included Eu, Lacy of Pontefract, Mandeville, Stafford, Tickhill and Warenne. The honors of Richmond and Paynel each owed fifty knights; among the lesser honors, Craon owed thirty knights, and the Braose honor of Bramber twenty-five. The original quotas are thought to have been arbitrary; some wealthy churches were given a slight burden. Peterborough Abbey's heavy burden may have been punitive, because Abbot Brand recognized Edgar the Atheling as king in 1066, though it is important to remember that this area was especially vulnerable, and that the imposition of a large *servitium debitum* on a particular monastery may have been dictated by necessity rather than by vengeance. Religious houses founded in William I's reign were not, as it were, brought into the scheme.

The fee became an important unit for financial purposes. From his tenants-in-chief the king could demand financial payments for traditional purposes; they, in turn, could make the same demands of their knightly tenants. An heir must pay relief before he could take over his lordship or fee. The tenant must give his lord financial aid on important social occasions. As royal and feudal administration grew more sophisticated these dues could be exploited to the crown's advantage. Early in the twelfth century the king began to raise scutage, taking money instead of service at a rate fixed for the occasion. For him the chief drawback of a feudal army was that service was due only for a limited period each year; this might have little relation to the length of a particular crisis or campaign. The advantage of commutation was that the king could hire mercenaries who would serve as long as the money to pay them was available.

For the English church the Norman conquest brought massive changes which, to contemporaries, were little short of disastrous. In the Confessor's reign the church still retained some of the strength engendered by the monastic reform movement of the tenth century. There were some thirty-five monasteries south of the Humber, a few sadly decayed but many flourishing. Peterborough enjoyed great material wealth, firm discipline and liturgical observance: these years were seen in retrospect as a golden age. The monks owed much to the patronage of Leofric, earl of Mercia, whose nephew, another Leofric, was abbot of Peterborough and of Burton, Coventry, Crowland and Thorney. The earl and his wife Godiva were generous supporters of the monastic order, founding the abbey at Coventry and making valuable gifts to half a dozen houses in the midlands. Other magnates worked on a small scale: Earl Odda founded a monastery at Great Malvern and built a chapel at Deerhurst in memory of his brother; Earl Harold established a community of secular canons at Waltham. The king himself was responsible for the new Romanesque church at Westminster Abbey.

One legacy of the work of the tenth-century reformers was the appointment to bishoprics of monks who could carry into the secular church the dedication, discipline and enthusiasm they had known in the cloister. Cnut and his advisers continued to recruit monastic bishops and the practice was maintained on a reduced scale by King Edward, though he also drew heavily on the secular clerks who served in his court and administration.

The Confessor reserved for himself the appointment of bishops. Only rarely did aristocratic influence secure a diocese for a candidate. Some of his nominees were foreign churchmen: Giso of Wells, Walter of Hereford and Herman of Ramsbury were from Lorraine, a notable centre of reform, and Leofric of Exeter was educated there. Robert of Jumièges, Ulf of Dorchester and William of London were Normans. Most of them were energetic bishops, aware of the reforming ideas current in the European church. Giso, Leofric and William reorganized their cathedral chapters, imposing a rule of life on their canons. The greater discipline they secured reflected a movement already gaining in popularity in Europe, the use of a quasi-monastic rule for communities of secular clerics. In the 1060s Aldred, archbishop of York, strengthened his diocese by establishing canons living under rule in his cathedral minster at York and in three large minster churches at Beverley, Ripon and Southwell.

Aldred was a bishop of wide experience. He was made abbot of Tavistock in 1027 and had been consecrated, probably as an assistant bishop, in the early 1040s. He became bishop of Worcester in 1046 and archbishop of York in 1061. He was a courtier bishop, keenly aware of the political value of serving the king; he was much concerned with royal business and especially with diplomacy. Widely travelled, he was perhaps the most cosmopolitan of the English bishops. He had no qualms about accepting the rewards such service could bring. There were precedents for holding the secure bishopric of Worcester with the poorly endowed diocese of York, and Aldred held both sees until 1062 when, on papal instructions, he was forced to give up Worcester. For exceptional reasons, in 1155 he was given charge of Hereford, and for a brief period he held three bishoprics. He also had the abbey of Winchcombe and was involved in an attempt to restore St Peter's, Gloucester.

His fellow archbishop, Stigand, began his career as a cleric in Cnut's service and was later closely associated with Queen Emma. Reading the signs of her declining influence, he moved into the circle of Earl Godwine, under whose patronage his service produced rich rewards. He was bishop of Elmham in 1043 and was translated to Winchester four years later. In the main political upheaval of the reign he was a spectator rather than a participant. The Norman monk Robert of Jumièges became an intimate and powerful adviser at the Confessor's court, where he emerged as a rival for power and a dangerous enemy of Earl Godwine. Edward made Robert bishop of London and, in 1051, archbishop of Canterbury, ignoring the claims of one of the earl's kinsmen. The exile of Godwine and his family in that year was the culmination of Robert's political manoeuvring and, when Godwine returned in 1052 and forced the king into submission, Robert fled to France. With the king's political position at its weakest and Godwine's advice the dominant factor, Stigand was intruded into the archbishopric of Canterbury, but he was never able to overcome the handicap of having taken the see belonging to Archbishop Robert. Successive attempts to secure papal approval of his appointment failed, and Stigand's position was weakened when he was given the symbol of his office, the *pallium*, by Benedict X, who was not recognized as being in the succession of lawful popes. These events vitiated Stigand's activities as archbishop. Until he had been given his *pallium*, newly appointed bishops preferred to go for conscration to one whose credentials were undisputed. Harold and William I were both crowned by Aldred, rather than risk a challenge to their title to the throne.

Even so, Stigand was potentially a dangerous man. He held Canterbury and Winchester together; he was said to have drawn revenues from a number of monasteries including Glastonbury, St Albans, St Augustine's at Canterbury and Ely, though the sequence of abbots at those monasteries does not allow a noticeably long interval between appointments. He retained a number of manors in his former bishopric of Elmham, leaving his successor a very impoverished diocese. He was wealthy; he controlled a substantial source of military power; he was a man of great guile and political experience. As nominal leader of the English church he brought it into great disrepute. Duke William was able to present himself to the papal curia as one who would remove a schismatic archbishop and bring the English church back into full orthodoxy. Aldred of York, the obvious person to maintain order and confidence in the English church, had to work under a grave disadvantage while Stigand was the man of influence at the king's court.

Politics and personalities present one problem as we review the impact of the Normans on the English church. Apart from politics and personalities, there was the difficult problem of a conflict of cultures. The English church was firmly Anglo-Saxon in its loyalties and its spirituality. The saints who were revered and whose shrines were honoured were uncompromisingly Anglo-Saxon; some of them were Celtic. The vernacular was widely used. There were strong local traditions in sculpture and manuscript illumination. English churchmen, especially in the south, were not unaware of what was happening in Europe: links between English and French monasteries were strong, as were links with Flanders and with Denmark and Norway; some of the cults observed in French churches were known in England. But the Anglo-Saxon traditions of the English church were not so well known outside England, and to the Normans the church in their newly conquered kingdom was local and remote; they gave it scant sympathy and thinly veiled contempt.

In Normandy the development of the church in the tenth century had been slow and unobtrusive, but an impetus for reform came in 1001 when William of Volpiano moved from Dijon to Fécamp and began the reform of that abbey. The monastic reform which spread over the whole duchy was closely linked with Cluny; it was highly centralized; it owed much to the patronage of the dukes of Normandy. Older monasteries, such as St Wandrille and Jumièges, were reformed, and new houses were founded. The monastery of Bec (now Le Bec Hellouin), which dates from 1039 – or perhaps more formally from the dedication of the church in 1041

– was to have a particular significance for Normandy and England. The secular church was also directly affected and the Norman bishoprics were revitalized. Bishops drawn from a varied but largely aristocratic background were concerned with rebuilding their cathedrals and organizing their chapters and administration. New monastic and cathedral churches were matched by many smaller parish churches. Under the duke's direct influence, church synods were held. All this was still developing in the 1060s and 1070s. Although it has often been overstated, there is an unmistakable contrast between the sense of decline evident in the English church and the sense of vigour and dynamism in the Norman church.

The Conqueror's early dealings with the church in England betray a note of caution. He was crowned by Aldred of York, whose death in 1069 removed a gifted supporter. Stigand was retained at Canterbury. He had been the first of the great English magnates to submit to William and he was either too dangerous or too useful to be discarded. In addition to his revenues from the church he is estimated to have had an annual income of £800 from his estates. Changes were made gradually while he was still holding Canterbury. Remigius, from Fécamp, was made bishop of Dorchester in 1067; in 1070 Thomas, a canon of Bayeux, was nominated to York, and Walkelin, one of the king's Norman chaplains, to Winchester. In that year the king secured papal support for sweeping changes. At a council held under the aegis of two papal legates, Archbishop Stigand and five other bishops were removed. Before the end of 1072 another three dioceses fell vacant. For Canterbury, William had already determined that Lanfranc, abbot of Caen, should become archbishop. Normans were appointed to Elmham, Exeter, Lichfield and Durham. For Chichester another Stigand was appointed; his background is obscure, but he is believed to have come from Normandy. The apparent uniformity of these Norman bishops conceals an interesting pattern of experience and loyalty. Walkelin of Winchester, Herfast of Elmham and Walcher of Durham were royal clerks serving in William's administration. Herfast had served him in Normandy before 1066. Osbern of Exeter, Peter of Lichfield and Stigand of Chichester were Normans who had been clerks in the Confessor's service. William continued to use them on his staff, and their bishoprics were rewards for long service. Osbern, brother of Earl William fitz Osbern, had spent many years in England and is sometimes described as the most anglicized of the Confessor's Norman friends. He had twenty-one years ahead of him as bishop before he died.

Lanfranc is the key figure. A teacher and scholar, not afraid of controversy, he withdrew to the abbey of Bec, where he lived as a simple cloister monk until he was coaxed back into active teaching. There he incurred the anger of Duke William, but from that unpropitious start the two men found a mutual respect. In 1063 William appointed him abbot of his new monastery St Stephen's, Caen. His move to Canterbury in 1070 renewed in England a working relationship that had been formed and tried in Normandy and the two men worked closely and harmoniously for the remainder of the reign. Both, for different reasons, were anxious to stress their autonomy in England, William as king and Lanfranc as metropolitan. The moral reform movement initiated by Pope Leo IX (1049–54) raised few problems for them. The accession of Gregory VII in 1073 put them under greater pressure. He strongly advocated that power lay with the papacy, not with metropolitical archbishops. Papal directives, the settlement of important cases at the papal curia, attendance at the councils called regularly by the reforming popes and the intrusion of papal legates were all part of the means by which this view of ecclesiastical authority could be enforced. Lanfranc, a metropolitan of the old school, much preferred to keep Pope Gregory at arm's length, paying lip-service to his authority, reducing to a minimum the occasions when it was exercised and pleading when necessary the pressure of royal control. As king, William had sound reasons for minimizing papal influence in his kingdom. His invasion of England had been given papal approval by Alexander II who had sent him a banner which was carried at the battle of Hastings. That was a symbol Gregory VII interpreted in feudal terms, while the king forthrightly rejected any claim that he held his kingdom as a papal fief.

Lanfranc's influence as metropolitan was enhanced in two ways. He insisted upon the obedience of all the bishops in his province and on his right to intervene when necessary in the affairs of their dioceses. He revived and regularly used the custom of exacting a written promise of obedience from each newly consecrated bishop. Where discipline was lax he was quick to condemn. At the same time, bishops consulted him when they were faced with problems. There was no simple collection of canon law that could be consulted, but Lanfranc had a personal collection of material he could use. His letters demonstrate clearly his skill in identifying the legal edicts and decisions which might apply in a given case and the force with which he could then prescribe the proper course of action. Lanfranc was responsible for establishing the principle that his authority extended over the whole of the English church. He ignored the fact that historically York was an independent province and he insisted that Thomas of Bayeux should promise obedience to Canterbury before he would consecrate him. Elsewhere, in his letters, he went further and declared that 'this whole island which is called Britain is within the undivided jurisdiction of our one church'. It was a claim heavy with consequences for Wales, Ireland and Scotland, as well as for northern England. He won a temporary victory over Thomas of Bayeux, but that was only one phase in a long battle. Discipline and training were brought together by the revival of provincial synods, where formal enactments could be made affecting the whole church, and of diocesan synods, where clergy could find firm guidance and mutual support. There could be no doubt that the English church was being brought up to date. Perhaps the most obvious sign of that was the transfer of cathedral churches to urban centres: Selsey to Chichester, Sherborne to Old Sarum – then little more than a fortified site – and Lichfield to Chester; and, at later dates, Dorchester to Lincoln, Wells to Bath, Thetford to Norwich and Chester to Coventry. Diocesan administration was extended with the widespread use of archdeacons, and the building up of a bishop's *familia*, his circle of clerks and advisers, can be discerned.

In the church, as in secular society, Englishmen were usually relegated to less important roles. Many survived in monasteries, where a small articulate minority maintained a tradition of English historical writing. At Worcester Cathedral Priory in the last decade of the eleventh century, Coleman wrote in Anglo-Saxon a biography of Bishop Wulfstan, later to be translated into Latin by the Anglo-Norman monk, William of Malmesbury. Another Englishman, John of Worcester, continued the Worcester tradition by maintaining a chronicle until 1141. A Peterborough monk continued one version of the Anglo-Saxon Chronicle until 1154. At Christ Church, Canterbury, Eadmer produced his *Life* of Archbishop Anselm and a study of recent events, his *Historia Novorum*. One of the most influential Englishmen of the twelfth century was Stephen Harding, from Sherborne, who became abbot of Cîteaux in 1109, and whose quiet genius provided a large part of the sound foundations for the Cistercian rule of life. Adelulf, prior of Nostell, was made bishop of Carlisle in 1133, and Henry Murdac, abbot of Fountains, became archbishop of York in 1147. All these may be exceptional cases, for they were men of influence. Most of them emerged from the large body of English monks surviving in the older-established Benedictine monasteries. But it is salutary to recall that Adelulf was Henry I's confessor and was prior of an Augustinian community founded about 1114; and Henry Murdac was a Cistercian.

The secular church gave fewer opportunities for Englishmen to hold responsible posts. French-speaking bishops needed *familiares* with whom they could talk easily and work without barriers. Even so, at Thetford, between 1090 and about 1120, Bondi was serving as dean and a fellow Englishman, Athselin, as provost. Within a few years, Salisbury had an English precentor, and in the 1120s an English schoolmaster was still in charge of education there. In the twelfth century the vast majority of English parishes were served by English priests. In areas like the Danelaw, where charters were issued and attested by the wealthier peasants, their names occur with frequency; elsewhere, they are identified on comparatively rare occasions.

Dynasties of hereditary priests were to be found in different parts of the country. In the 1130s one member of such a family, Beohrtric, the vicar of a Somerset parish, was still a monoglot Englishman, and he found the lack of even the most rudimentary knowledge of French and Latin a handicap. Two distinguished writers were the product of such clerical families. Ailred, who became abbot of Rievaulx in 1147, was the son of the last of a line of hereditary priests of Hexham, and his response to the challenges of a different culture and of the complexity of frontier society was both positive and subtle. As an Englishman he came to terms with Norman domination; as a Northumbrian he found a rewarding career in the service of the king of Scotland; as a monk he found fulfilment and security at the Cistercian abbey of Rievaulx, and there, too, he became a writer of more than local importance. Ralph of Diss (*de Diceto*) had a long career at St Paul's, London, as archdeacon of Middlesex (1152–*c*.1181) and dean (*c*.1181–1202); he was the son of Ulfketel, a hereditary priest in Norfolk. They do not stand alone. Another chronicler, Roger of Howden, despite his French Christian name, was the last of his family to be hereditary priest at Howden.

There were others of mixed parentage, best represented by two writers in whose works English and Norman traditions were fused and maintained, William of Malmesbury and Orderic Vitalis. They can be matched from Wales by Gerald of Wales, much less perceptive than Orderic and less disciplined by far than William, but still a writer who had somehow to live with the conflicting claims and loyalties created by intermarriage.

3

The Resistance of the Welsh

For much of the eleventh century Welsh princes and English magnates lived in a state of open conflict or uneasy truce. The kings of the West Saxon dynasty had claimed to be overlords of Welsh rulers and Welsh territory, and from the reign of Alfred their patronage and influence became more than a formality. The earls of Mercia and their kinsmen campaigned in Wales. Welsh and English contested the control of lands west of the Wye and the Dee. The linear frontier between England and Wales was defined by Offa's dyke, but there was no sharp divide between English and Welsh culture. A shifting tide of conquest and settlement created a bewildering pattern along the frontier.

Wales itself was a land of many kingdoms. A powerful dynasty was established in the northern kingdom of Gwynedd. The influence of the dynasty ruling in Powys was often limited; the kingdom was frequently under pressure from Gwynedd on the Welsh side and from powerful English magnates to the east. In south Wales, in the kingdom of Deheubarth, successive rulers maintained their authority until the end of the twelfth century, albeit with restricted frontiers. Lesser dynasties ruled smaller territories, notably in Brycheiniog and Morgannwg and in different parts of Gwent. Morgannwg covered a large area in the south-east, and its coastline along the Bristol Channel provided the opportunity for contact and trade. Brecon and Brecknock, Gwent, and Dyfed (formerly

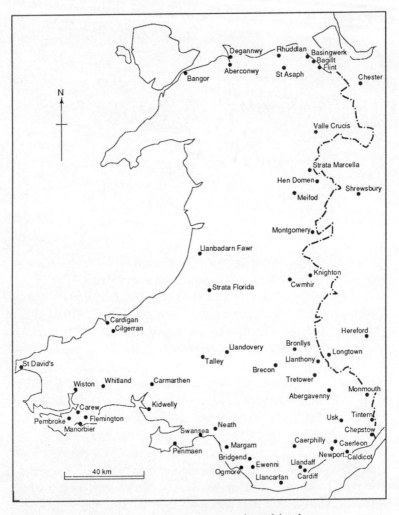

Map 2   Wales: principal places mentioned in the text

a kingdom in west Wales) remain as familiar place-names in modern Wales, and Morgannwg was preserved in the lordship of Glamorgan. By contrast, Deheubarth has not survived in modern use, and local names in south-east Wales, Glywysing and Gwynllŵg, once significant political units, are, like many Welsh place-names, unfamiliar to a wide readership outside the principality.

In each kingdom it was rare to find a succession of strong leaders. Strife between siblings was endemic, and since different septs within one dynasty retained claims to succession a challenge for power could come from a wide range of individuals. Chroniclers recorded many instances of assassination, blinding and mutilation as hazards of family life within the royal kindred. Warfare, raiding and plundering were rife. A powerful king could exert a strong influence in kingdoms other than his own, and on rare occasions one ruler could establish his authority over much, if not all, of Wales. In the ninth century, Rhodri Mawr – Rhodri the Great – ruled Gwynedd and Powys in the north and extended his power over a wide swathe of territory in west and south Wales. His grandson Hywel Dda – Hywel the Good – established himself in south Wales and, late in life, secured Gwynedd and Powys. It is dangerously easy to underestimate the political skill and strength of individual rulers and to emphasize elements of weakness and instability in the history of different kingdoms. Hywel's qualities as a ruler can be discerned from the range of territories he ruled and from the codification of Welsh laws associated with his name. In a different context, a pilgrimage to Rome and close contact with the English kings Athelstan and Edward the Elder, forged at their insistence, gave him a range of experience outside Wales unusual in a Welsh ruler.

In the middle decades of the eleventh century the prospect of both strong government and political unity emerged again. In 1039, a young princeling, Gruffydd ap Llywelyn, succeeded to the kingdom of Gwynedd. From the outset it was clear that his ambition was to secure south Wales (the kingdom of Deheubarth), and before the year was over he had driven Hywel ab Edwin out of that kingdom. But it would take many campaigns to impose his authority there. Hywel survived and he and his successor, Gruffydd ap Rhydderch, maintained the integrity of Deheubarth until 1055. Gruffydd ap Rhydderch's roots lay in south-east Wales, and he pursued an active policy against the English, diverting an attack by a Scandinavian force away from their first targets in south Wales to Gwent and the English bank of the Wye and, on a later occasion, breaching the defences of Herefordshire and striking deep into the settled areas of the shire.

His death in 1055 gave Gruffydd ap Llywelyn the chance to achieve his long-term ambition and to rule a united Wales. Walter Map, writing in the reign of Henry II, was aware of traditions about him which appear to be authentic and which emphasize the treachery, ruthlessness and harsh measures by which he imposed his authority. Gruffydd remains a very significant figure in eleventh-century Wales. Between 1055 and 1063 he used his strength to pursue an aggressive policy against the English, raiding the southern borders, plundering Hereford and destroying its cathedral. In 1055 and again in 1058 he was drawn into alliance with the family of the earls of Mercia, who also secured support from Scandinavian seafarers; they saved Earl Aelfgar from political eclipse and frustrated attempts by the sons of Earl Godwine to extend their domination of the Confessor's kingdom. Gruffydd maintained his pressure on the frontiers, testing the English resources to the limit, until his overthrow and death in 1063.

The scale of his success has been seen in tenurial changes along the frontier. In the tenth century, English settlers farmed lands along the Welsh coast of the Dee estuary as far north as Rhuddlan, in an area which formed the hundred of Atiscross. Rhuddlan itself was the site of an Anglo-Saxon *burh*. On the borders of Cheshire and Shropshire the English had established the hundreds of Exestan and Mersete in Welsh territory. By 1063, Gruffydd controlled all these areas, and his success is symbolized by the fact that he established a *llys*, a palace, at Rhuddlan. Along the central stretch of the frontier, land associated with Knighton, Kington, Radnor and Huntington had passed from English into Welsh hands. In the south, where the successes of Gruffydd ap Rhydderch were a significant factor, Ewyas and Erging (Archenfield), both disputed territories, lay outside the jurisdiction of Herefordshire.

All this made Gruffydd a dangerous enemy for the Confessor and his immediate advisers, who tried a number of expedients to defend the weak Anglo-Welsh border. One consequence was that in 1053 Edward appointed his nephew Ralph as earl of Hereford; he raised a castle at Hereford and began the experiment of using a cavalry force to defend the frontier, where they suffered a humiliating defeat at their first main test. A militant bishop of Hereford, Leofgar, suffered a crushing repulse, with heavy losses, at Gruffydd's hands, and the bishop of Worcester was drafted in as a senior statesman-administrator to restore stability. Finally in the winter months of 1062–3, Earl Harold made a surprise attack on Rhuddlan but Gruffydd was able to escape by sea. Not to be thwarted, Harold and his brother Tostig attacked in force in the summer, and this time Gruffydd fled inland. In this crisis he was put to death by Welshmen: old enemies have long memories!

The power Gruffydd ap Llywelyn had built up in Wales was quickly dispersed, partly under English influence. His half-brothers, children of his mother's second marriage, succeeded him; Bleddyn ap Cynfyn in Gwynedd and Rhiwallon ap Cynfyn in Powys. In the south the dispossessed dynasties were restored in Deheubarth and, with minor but potentially dangerous adjustments, Gwynllŵg and Morgannwg. Harold followed up his success with a campaign in Gwent. This has been taken to imply that he brought that territory under his lordship, though it may have been little more than a move to limit Caradog ap Gruffydd ap Rhydderch to Gwynllŵg. Harold felt sufficiently secure to build a hunting lodge to the west of the Wye at Portskewett, but as soon as it was finished Caradog swooped and destroyed it. In terms of the Welsh past the eclipse of Gruffydd ap Llywelyn signalled a return to a familiar pattern, but in terms of the immediate future it meant that any threat from the Normans established in England in 1066 would have to be met by new and untried men.

In his earliest years, William the Conqueror made provision for the defence of especially vulnerable areas of the kingdom. On the southern stretch of the Welsh frontier he established William fitz Osbern as earl of Hereford with Hereford as his main base. The fact that he made this outpost the centre of his activities in the west midlands is a strong indication of his commission to defend the

weak borders of Herefordshire and Gloucestershire. He strengthened the defences of Herefordshire with castles at Wigmore and
Ewyas. At Ewyas he established a new castle and gave four
carucates of waste land to Walter de Lacy, a tenure from which the
castle took its name of Ewyas Lacy; and he re-established the castle
raised in the Confessor's reign in the neighbouring territory of
Ewyas Harold. By 1086 Roger de Lacy had built up a new lordship
at Ewyas Lacy. At Clifford, fitz Osbern built a castle on waste land;
it lay within the English kingdom but it was not in any hundred and
it paid no customary dues. On the Wye, he set up the castle at
Monmouth, where the danger might come from the Welshmen of
Gwent Uwchcoed.

In the south, working from Gloucestershire, fitz Osbern built a
castle at Strigoil (Chepstow) on the Welsh bank of the Wye and, no
longer content with defence, began the process of extending
Norman control into Gwent. The land that was annexed formed
the castlery of Strigoil, and beyond that, extending to the Usk (and
breaking beyond that barrier), was a second castlery held by
Turstin, son of Rolf, based on Caerleon; it paid a number of its dues
in 1086 through Chepstow and the sheriff of Gloucestershire.

In times of crisis fitz Osbern was much in demand in other parts
of the kingdom and he must have relied heavily on capable subor-
dinates. Domesday Book offers some clues as to who they were and
gives more information about the efficient way in which they organized the earl's estates. Roger de Pîtres, recruited from fitz
Osbern's Norman estates in Pacy, served the earl in Gloucestershire and in the castlery of Chepstow. Ralph de Bernay, drawn from
an area where fitz Osbern had many interests, served him in
Herefordshire, and he too held land in Chepstow. Both men were
sheriffs, serving the king long after fitz Osbern had died. Their
local knowledge must lie behind much of the earl's estate manage-
ment and his disposition of castles and forces.

Earl William died early in 1071. In the last four years of his life
he left his mark on Herefordshire and Gloucestershire and the
neighbouring Welsh territories in Gwent. That he was a man of
great power on the border cannot be doubted. Christopher Lewis
(1984) has argued with some speculation that the extent of his

authority and the range of powers he exercised were more limited than earlier writers have allowed (Wightman, 1966; Walker, 1978b). He has also reopened the question of the standing and function of the greatest Norman magnates in the Conqueror's reign (Lewis, 1991). But, whatever the legal niceties, fitz Osbern was a man wielding great authority. It has been suggested that the Conqueror wanted him to fill the role played by Earl Harold in the Confessor's reign.

William fitz Osbern's brief career in England initiated many important developments, but it also left a number of important questions unanswered. He was succeeded in England by his second son, Roger de Breteuil, who survived for four years before he rebelled against the Conqueror in 1075 and was deprived of his lands and his earldom. He was not given the wide authority his father had enjoyed, and he resented that. There are indications that he was active in the castlery of Chepstow and that he and his men were tempted to take part in the struggle for power between Welsh claimants to Gwent in 1072. Some of his knights found a refuge west of the Usk when he was disgraced in 1075. The disappearance of this powerful family was one factor that gave the rulers of south Wales a respite from pressure and conquest until the end of the Conqueror's reign.

Early in 1070 the king gave control of Chester to Gherbod, a Fleming. We know little about him and we cannot gauge what particular ability he might have brought to the frontier zone, nor what the king intended him to do there. He withdrew from England, and the king had to rethink his plans for the settlement of this area. He was followed by Hugh of Avranches, who held the earldom of Chester for more than thirty years. We do not know how soon after Gherbod's departure he was appointed, but the conditions on which he held Cheshire suggest an early date. With one important exception, the shire was held by Earl Hugh and his men, all of whom held their lands of the earl. The exception was that the bishop of Chester held of the king all the lands that belonged to his bishopric. The third magnate with extensive lands on the frontier was Roger of Montgomery who was given the earldom of Shrewsbury, probably as early as 1068 (Lewis, 1991). He held the

earldom for twenty-six years and was succeeded by his younger son
Hugh, who died in 1098. Then Robert of Bellême – the elder son
who had inherited the family's Norman lands – took over the
English inheritance, which he held until his disgrace and fall in
1102. In both Chester and Shrewsbury the first Norman earl had
many years in which to pursue a policy of advance and aggrandize-
ment in Wales.

The opportunities for intervention were created by the political
and military ambitions of a number of rival Welsh princes. The two
brothers Bleddyn of Gwynedd and Rhiwallon of Powys maintained
a close family alliance and joined forces to attack Deheubarth in
1070, and in the campaign that followed Rhiwallon was killed, and
Bleddyn took over Powys. In 1075 Bleddyn himself was killed,
again in conflict with Deheubarth, and his sons were passed over
in favour of a cousin, Trahaearn ap Caradog, whose ambitions
were greater than his actual political strength. He was challenged
from an unexpected quarter. In 1039, when Iago of Gwynedd was
murdered, his son Cynan had taken refuge in Ireland. There he
married the granddaughter of Sitric, king of Dublin, and their
son Gruffydd was born and grew to manhood.

He chose the political crisis of 1075 to make a bid for power in
Wales. In Gwynedd he could appeal to the older traditions of his
dynasty, but his strength depended upon a personal bodyguard –
his *teulu* – of Irish fighters and an opportunist alliance with
Norman forces from Rhuddlan, neither of which were popular in
Gwynedd. In the short term, although his control over Gwynedd
was disputed, Trahaearn could win the advantage. In south Wales,
Caradog ap Gruffydd ap Rhydderch and a claimant with much less
political experience, Rhys ap Tewdwr, were engaged in a similar
struggle for power. These conflicts were clarified at the battle of
Mynydd Carn in 1078, when Trahaearn and Caradog were killed
and their rivals left in stronger, though not unassailable, positions
as Gruffydd ap Cynan soon learned. Having used Normans from
Rhuddlan as allies, he made the mistake of launching an attack on
that stronghold. At the first opportunity, he was taken by the earl of
Chester, and kept as a prisoner for many years.

These were the conditions in which rapid and extensive advances could be made from Chester into north Wales under Earl Hugh and his cousin Robert of Rhuddlan. Neither of them emerge as attractive personalities; the earl was a *bon viveur*, gross in appearance, whose hunting Orderic described as a daily devastation of his lands, and whose household included a dangerous force of young fighting men lacking almost all moral restraint. Robert earned an unenviable reputation for ruthless and brutal treatment of the Welsh. He made the castle at Rhuddlan and the outpost he built at Degannwy centres from which he could dominate his acquisitions in the area formerly settled by the English, and from which he could make some advances into Gwynedd. Rhuddlan was held jointly by the earl and Robert of Rhuddlan, who shared the revenues from the borough they established there. They gave the burgesses the favourable customs which prevailed at Breteuil and Hereford. In 1086 Robert owed the king £40 for *Nortwales*; that this meant the kingdom of Gwynedd is made clear in Domesday Book by the statement that Robert claimed (against the earl of Shrewsbury) the territory of *Arvester*, the *cantref* of Arwystli, an outlying territory of that kingdom. It has to be said that in seeking so great an advance along the north coast of Wales the Normans stretched their resources to the limit. Without reinforcements on a substantial scale their hopes of retaining all their acquisitions were not very strong.

Further south, Roger of Montgomery's advances assumed a different pattern. From Shrewsbury, he and his military tenants built up lordships on the English side of the frontier and recovered areas that had passed into Welsh hands, reclaiming Oswestry and the hundred of Mersete. They went further and secured, at least for temporary occupation, the Welsh territories of Edeirnion and Cynllaith; in an area which fell more conveniently to the earls of Chester, they took Iâl and handed it over to Hugh of Avranches. The symbol of their threat to Wales was the motte and bailey castle Hen Domen, which Earl Roger raised at the place to which he gave the name of his Norman *caput*, Montgomery. A decade later, they would break out and make west Wales their particular target.

The earldom of Shrewsbury has a special interest for Anglo-Norman historians because it makes explicit what must be inferred elsewhere on the frontier. In fitz Osbern's territory we may assume the role of Roger de Pîtres, and in north Wales we may come close to understanding the relative positions of Earl Hugh and Robert of Rhuddlan. With the earldom of Shrewsbury, which he knew well, Orderic Vitalis provides us with clear and detailed information. Earl Roger could not deal personally with the whole range of administration and expansion in his border lordship. He appointed Warin the Bald as his sheriff, 'employing him to crush the Welsh and other opponents and pacify the whole province placed under his rule'. Warin was a close adviser of the earl, who endowed him with estates in Shropshire, and who, to mark his responsibilities and status, gave him a niece, Amieria, as his wife. One foray he made into Welsh territory was mentioned in the *Life* of Gruffydd ap Cynan. He acquired land in the hundred of Mersete, though it was his successor who built the castle at Oswestry as the centre of the Norman lordship. Warin's death in 1085 may mark the first phase of recovery and conquest. His son Hugh was then a minor, who had to wait until 1098 before he was given his father's office of sheriff. In the mean time Earl Roger appointed another tenant from his Norman lordship, Reginald de Bailleul, as sheriff and he, too, married Amieria.

By the 1080s royal interest in Wales had become a factor of some importance. In 1081 the Conqueror travelled with a substantial force through south Wales as far as St David's. It was presented as a pilgrimage, and should almost certainly be seen as a show of force, though how it would compare with the scale of William's expedition to Scotland in 1072 cannot be determined. We must assume that in 1081 William established an accord with Rhys ap Tewdwr of Deheubarth. In Domesday Book Rhys was said to hold his kingdom for an annual payment of £40, and that indicates both an agreement and a formal submission by the Welsh prince, who became in effect a client king. This was another important factor in producing a period of comparative peace on the southern frontier, and Norman advances into Wales were not resumed until after the Conqueror's death. Then, in a renewed burst of activity in the reign of William Rufus, Norman attacks on the frontier were resumed. From the earldom of Shrewsbury there were bold sweeps into west and south-west Wales; Bernard of Neufmarché was active in Brycheiniog and Robert fitz Hamo in Morgannwg.

The centre of fitz Hamo's activities was the castle at Cardiff, where the ruins of a Roman fort were used as the outer defences, with a large motte, surrounded by a deep ditch, as the inner stronghold. The initial expansion of Norman control in Morgannwg, as far west as the river Ogmore, was achieved by Robert fitz Hamo before 1104. It was extended westwards by his son-in-law Robert, earl of Gloucester, who carried Norman control as far as Neath, and whose advances in Wales belong largely to the reign of Henry I. Advances into the hill country to the north and the gradual extension of Norman authority there was a long process, still to be completed in the thirteenth century.

The castle at Cardiff has normally been regarded as fitz Hamo's work. One tradition, however, asserted that Cardiff was founded by William the Conqueror in 1081, and for long that was regarded as a view which should not be ignored, but which could not be substantiated. In recent studies, the case for an early date for the foundation of Cardiff castle has been argued very forcibly. It turns chiefly on a reappraisal of numismatic evidence by G. C. Boon (1986), whose case has won wide acceptance. Coins of William I, struck at Cardiff, some before 1083 and others between 1083 and 1086, indicate a Norman base there well before any link with Robert fitz Hamo can be established. If that is sound, the Conqueror's journey to Wales in 1081 is the obvious occasion for the mint to be established and used. In the past, the identification of this mint met with strong reservations but Boon has presented a persuasive case for accepting it. He has also suggested that it may have been a branch of the mint at Bristol.

Those whose interests lie in castles have made a number of tentative suggestions which have more of speculation than justifiable conclusion about them (cf. Spurgeon, 1987). They have argued that the size of the motte at Cardiff implies a royal foundation and that smaller mottes in the area could perhaps date from the Conqueror's reign. The case is also linked with the possibility – to be treated with great caution – that a mint was set up at St David's at the same time. The whole exercise is an interesting example of how numismatists, archaeologists and historians can combine to reopen and re-examine a familiar problem for which only scanty evidence exists. Apart from the element of speculation, difficult issues arise when questions of motive are considered. That a mint should be set up in a newly established castle at Cardiff instead of in a borough in secure territory as close as Gwent is a curious feature. That the king should take with him on campaign, or summon to him in the course of a campaign, a moneyer with his equipment and materials is in itself exceptional. That the king should need to mint coins in Wales requires some explanation. Suggestions range from the Conqueror's need to find money to pay his army in Wales to the necessity for Rhys ap Tewdwr to have access to acceptable coinage in order to pay his annual render of £40 for Deheubarth. Neither invites much confidence. But, despite these problems, the striking of coins at Cardiff castle in or soon after 1081 must be taken seriously and that involves some reassessment of long-standing views of the early history of the lordship of Glamorgan.

In the last years of the eleventh century and the first decades of the twelfth, the Normans made considerable advances in south Wales. Bernard of Neufmarché was active in Brycheiniog in the late 1080s. He established his principal castle at Brecon and in 1093, not far from his castle, he defeated Rhys ap Tewdwr in a decisive battle in which Rhys was killed. With his death, the kingdom of Deheubarth was left without effective defence against its enemies, Welsh and Norman alike. In Brycheiniog, Bernard's military tenants held lands and castles to safeguard the lordship, with the Picards at Tretower, the Revels at Hay, and the Turbervilles at Crickhowell. The fitz Pons family, established at Clifford, from which they took their name, were given Bronllys.

From Shrewsbury, Norman forces had attacked Ceredigion and Dyfed in 1073–4, in what might best be described as exploratory probes. After the death of Rhys ap Tewdwr, Earl Roger mounted a major invasion of Ceredigion, established a castle at the place that would later be called Cardigan and swept south to build a castle at Pembroke, where his younger son, Arnulf, was left in command. At another key position, William Rufus established the sheriff of Devon, William, son of Baldwin, who had a castle on the river Towy at Rhyd y Gors; the link that he and his brother established between south Wales and Devonshire helps to explain Norman immigration across the Bristol Channel (Rowlands, 1981). At a later date the centre of Norman power was transferred further up the river from Rhyd y Gors to Carmarthen.

Norman settlements in north and south Wales were challenged between 1094 and 1098 when Welsh forces rallied and mounted a very effective counter-attack. In the north, Robert of Rhuddlan was killed and the Normans were driven out of the northern reaches of Gwynedd. Gruffydd ap Cynan began the slow process of re-establishing himself in Gwynedd. The river Conwy became the line of demarcation between Welsh and Norman power. Cadwgan ap Bleddyn of Powys was the most prominent Welsh leader until his death in 1111, while Gruffydd was laying the foundations for a long and influential reign. The earldom of Chester passed to a young boy in 1102, and, with the earldom of Shrewsbury in eclipse, English aggression was much reduced. To control the land between the Conwy and the Clwyd became increasingly an ambition for the princes of Gwynedd and Powys and the earls of Chester to pursue.

Elsewhere, under extreme pressure between 1094 and 1096, the Normans were driven back into their castles. In Brycheiniog, under heavy attack the castles 'remained intact with their garrisons in them'. In Dyfed, Pembroke held out, and Rhyd y Gors only surrendered when its castellan died.

Henry I made his influence felt very forcibly in Wales. His accession had been opposed by Robert of Bellême, and in 1102 Henry determined to break him and his family. His lands in England were reclaimed, his control of Shropshire and the midland stretch of the frontier was brought to an end, and a leading royal administrator was made responsible for the whole area. His brother Arnulf shared in his eclipse and, deprived of Pembroke, took refuge in Ireland. The most notable of those who had held subordinate positions in his Welsh territories and who emerged with enhanced power was Gerald of Windsor, constable of Pembroke castle and lord of Carew. Cemais was granted to a Somerset family, the fitz

Martins, and Ceredigion to Gilbert fitz Richard of Clare. The king was directly responsible for the settlement of Flemish pioneers over a wide area of Dyfed. They gave their name to Flemington and Wizo, their 'prince', gave his name to the castle and settlement at Wiston.

Recognizing Carmarthen as a crucial site, Henry established there a trusted royal official, Walter of Gloucester, through whom he could exercise direct influence in south Wales. Further east, Kidwelly was given to Roger, bishop of Salisbury, and before the end of the reign it had passed to the family of de Londres; Gower was given to the earl of Warwick. In Brycheiniog he ensured an acceptable succession by giving Bernard of Neufmarché's daughter, with her father's lands, in marriage to Miles of Gloucester. Ewyas Lacy the king gave to another curial official, Payn fitz John. Morgannwg was secured for the king's bastard son Robert (later earl of Gloucester), through marriage with the daughter and heiress of Robert fitz Hamo. To curb Welsh rulers Henry mounted two campaigns in Wales, in 1114 and 1121. Rees Davies (1985) has emphasized the fact that Henry was more deeply involved in Welsh affairs than any English king before the reign of Edward I. Like his father and his brother, he was concerned to show that Norman magnates were not free to do as they liked in Wales, but were subject to the king's will. He also secured the recognition in more explicit terms of his rights of overlordship in Powys and Gwynedd.

There is another strand in this pattern of Norman settlement. In Wales, as in Scotland, settlers could move from one area to another and extend their stakes in the country, a process that Barrow (1980) describes as internal colonization, and that Davies (1990) and Bartlett (1993) describe as internal expansion. We cannot always determine why they were tempted, nor by what means they acquired new lordships. The family of fitz Pons were settled in the northern stretch of the lordship of Brecknock, which included the old Welsh centre at Talgarth. Their castle at Bronllys lay well away from the settlement. They extended their interest further to the west, invading and settling in Cantref Bychan, where they built their principal castle at Llandovery. Henry I appears to have given his approval to this *fait accompli*, but the initiative seems to have been with the settlers, not with the king. The family which took its name from Barry, on the coast of Glamorgan, moved west to Dyfed and acquired Manorbier. Marriage links meant that they were closely associated with their new lordship, and Manorbier was the family home for Gerald of Wales and his brothers.

One of Robert fitz Hamo's military tenants was William de Londres, who was given the lordship of Ogmore. The castle he established there was extended by his successors, who built the fine stone keep before the end of the twelfth century. His son Maurice was responsible for the Romanesque church at Ewenni, which he gave to St Peter's Abbey, Gloucester, and endowed as a priory. There he was buried, and his family continued to be closely associated with the lordship well into the thirteenth century. But at some stage during the reign of Henry I they acquired the Welsh territories of Cydweli and Carnwyllion. These western territories contributed to the family's wealth, notably by the flocks of sheep that could be reared there, though they were rarely mentioned in the surviving records. They remained with the de Londres heirs until Hawise de Londres, already twice widowed, married Patrick de Chaworth, in or about 1216. She lived until 1274, and soon after her death her sons divided her inheritance. Her eldest son, already closely associated with Kidwelly and its concentric castle, retained the western lordships, and Ogmore was given to his younger brother.

By 1135, when Henry I died, the general pattern of Norman lordships in Wales had been established, though there were to be changes in the second half of the twelfth century. The accession of Stephen was the occasion for a widespread reassertion of Welsh power. Gower was attacked, and the Normans lost control of Ceredigion and Cantref Bychan; in the north Oswestry and the disputed territory between the Dee and the Conwy were reclaimed by the Welsh. As close to the border as the lordship of Abergavenny, Richard fitz Gilbert could be ambushed and killed by Morgan ab Owain, the leading figure in the Welsh dynasty of Gwynllŵg. After Henry II's accession, a number of these territories were recovered and the full pressure of royal authority was restored.

Increasingly the Norman lordships in Wales reflected changes brought about by marriage and political hazards. In 1155 Roger, earl of Hereford, rebelled against Henry II; he surrendered without a struggle and died a few months later. His successors lost the earldom and many valuable estates, and they fell back on Caldicot, Brecknock and Abergavenny, with only a shadow of the power once wielded by their father, Miles of Gloucester. A decade later, the last male heir of Earl Miles was dead, and the family's estates were divided between three co-heiresses. One result was the establishment of the Braose family in Brecknock and Abergavenny; their tenure was broken in 1207 when King John's powerful former favourite, William de Braose, fled first to Ireland and then to France. His Welsh lordships were seized and were not restored to his heirs until 1218.

The Clares had grown rich through the patronage of Henry I, and among the estates granted to them were lands in Gwent forfeited by Roger de Breteuil. These were given to Walter de Clare, who was established in Chepstow, Caerleon and Usk. When he died without a son to inherit, these lands passed to a nephew, himself a younger son; to this unexpected inheritance King Stephen added Pembroke and the earldom of Pembroke. All these passed to Richard fitz Gilbert (Strongbow) in 1153, and eventually to his daughter and her husband William Marshal. Henry II did not suppress the earldom of Pembroke, little though he liked Stephen's creations, but his attitude was markedly ambiguous. Immediately after his accession in 1189 Richard I gave Isabel, Strongbow's heiress, with her rich inheritance, to William Marshal. Chroniclers of Richard I's reign refer to William as earl of Strigoil, and in 1197 John, as lord of Ireland, allowed him to attest two charters as earl. On one occasion in that year he witnessed a charter of Richard I as Earl William; with that exception the king did not recognize his status, and the earldom was not formally conferred on him until John's accession in 1199.

The most striking development occurred in west Wales. There, at the beginning of the twelfth century, Gerald of Windsor, constable of Pembroke castle, had married Nest, daughter of Rhys ap Tewdwr of Deheubarth. Their eldest son succeeded Gerald as lord of Carew; a younger son, David, was bishop of St David's; their daughter Angharad married William de Barry of Manorbier. Nest also had children fathered by Henry I and Stephen, constable of Cardigan castle; of her sons and grandsons, three inherited established lordships in south Wales, and another eight were familiar though not well-endowed figures on the March. Here were the reserves of manpower on which Strongbow could draw for his Irish venture.

This dynasty was particularly significant because of its mixed racial and cultural inheritance. Nest was the daughter of a powerful and successful prince of Deheubarth, and, as her grandson Gerald of Wales frequently made clear, her Welsh blood and royal descent were a source of pride for the family. The appointment of her son David as bishop of St David's in 1148 owed much to strong local influence, and the links between the bishopric and the ruling dynasty of Deheubarth might be considered dangerous. Again, Gerald of Wales makes it clear that such speculations were current at the court of Henry II. Here, as in Gwent, was a marcher family of whom the king had cause to feel suspicious.

With a minority of settlers in control, how did Welsh and Normans coexist? Compared with the late thirteenth and fourteenth centuries there is very little evidence to consult. In the castleries of Chepstow and Caerleon in 1086 there was a mixture of manorial farms and dairy farms, which point to a traditional Welsh pastoral economy. Villages with Welsh reeves made renders in kind, providing honey, pigs and cows. At the same time, there were estates assessed by carucates and under the plough on the pattern of manorial estates in England: one lay on the Welsh side of the Usk, and English practice prevailed there. At Caerwent, Jocelyn the Breton had five carucates with two ploughs, and two Welshmen worked the estate. When the hundred of Mersete, in Shropshire, was reclaimed from Welsh control, Domesday Book recorded a normal manorial economy. But in a dozen manors, the workforce was made up of Welshmen. At Maesbury, for example, ten Welshmen and a priest had eight ploughs; at Halston two Welshmen and a Frenchman had one and a half ploughs. The exceptional entries record that Tudor, a Welshman, held a Welsh district, or that Madoc held Halston and Burtone, or that Edeirnion rendered eight cows a year from the Welshmen there, or that at Kinnerly a Welshman rendered one hawk a year for his tenement. With a change of political control, the Welshmen living in that area stayed to cultivate the land, with most of them working under English rather than Welsh conditions. In the estates held by Normans in north Wales under the earl of Chester, there is no indication that Welsh tenure or a Welsh labour force survived.

What is far more significant, though it is sometimes difficult to discern, is the uneasy balance in which new Norman lords and the old Welsh ruling elite lived together. It is clear that the settlers took over the richer farming lands of the river valleys and imposed a manorial pattern on them, while the Welsh were relegated to the uplands where they could follow their traditional pastoral routine. But that obscures the strength of the Welsh presence and the effectiveness of their opposition to the invaders. They were never divorced from their Welsh compatriots living beyond the areas of Norman settlement.

Some illustrations may point to the scale of their activities. In the lordship of Kidwelly Welsh attacks on the castle there were a recurrent feature throughout the twelfth and thirteenth centuries. In Ceredigion an early Norman occupation marked by the establishment of a number of castles was overthrown in Stephen's reign, and the Clares could not muster the strength to achieve a permanent recovery of their lost lordship. In Gwent rival Welsh princelings struggled for power, and nearby in Gwynllŵg the ruling dynasty survived and could take the initiative in curbing Norman expansion. The lordship of Glamorgan demonstrates the strength of Welsh survival more clearly than many lordships on the March. In Gwynllŵg, the grandson of Gruffydd ap Rhydderch, Morgan ab Owain, was an influential magnate. He made terms with the Norman settlers, and was to be found in the retinue of Robert, earl of Gloucester, whose charters he attested using the style 'Morgan the king'. When the monarchy was weakened in England, he pursued an independent policy, and was responsible for ambushing and killing Richard fitz Gilbert near Crickhowell in 1136. His family remained strong throughout the thirteenth century and produced a leader of revolt against the earl of Gloucester in 1294 who could play politics with sufficient skill to secure a pardon from Edward I.

The leading figure in the dynasty of Morgannwg was Iestyn ap Gwrgant, whose sons controlled the lordships of Neath and Afan and the hill country of the northern territories of Glamorgan, later to be identified as the manors of Glynrhondda and Meisgyn. A second dynasty was established in Senghennydd in the middle of the twelfth century by Ifor ap Meurig, better known by his nick-name of Ifor Bach. In 1158 he attacked Cardiff castle, entered it by stealth and carried off Earl William of Gloucester and his family. His successors continued to harass the lords of Glamorgan throughout the thirteenth century, and in 1267 his great-grandson Gruffydd ap Rhys was captured by the earl of Gloucester, Gilbert the Red, and taken off to Kilkenny to be kept in custody there. In the lordships of Brecknock and Abergavenny, relations between the Braoses and local Welsh leaders were stormy and violent, with the massacre of Seisyll ap Dyfnwal and his companions at Abergavenny in 1175 and the execution of Trahaearn Fychan in 1197. Later, when the Bohuns inherited Brecknock, a different pattern prevailed, and the leading Welsh dynasty provided a series of able administrators to organize the lordship for them.

The Welsh leaders of the twelfth century did not act in isolation. They were under the protection of the prince of Deheubarth, and from 1155 until 1197 that kingdom was ruled by Rhys ap Gruffydd – the Lord Rhys. He defied Henry II's attempts to reduce his power and to dislodge him, and he brought Henry to the point of a major change of policy in Wales. At first the king encouraged the barons of the southern March to oppose Rhys and to check his activities. Then, as Strongbow's invasion of Ireland was being planned, Henry found it politic to reach accord with Rhys in order to check the independence of the marcher lords. The politics of the March were never simple, and the interplay between the king, the Welsh princes, marcher lords and local Welsh dynasties was intricate and subtle.

Under these conditions the Welsh church was transformed in structure, function and personnel. Diocesan organization was closely linked with a shifting pattern of political power. The traditions of the medieval church were drawn from the age of the saints, missionary clerics who preached a new faith in Wales; the churches they and their disciples founded were important centres of worship and they preserve in their dedications the names of many early saints who would otherwise remain unknown. Early churches dedicated to saints such as Beuno, David, Deiniol, Padarn and Teilo demonstrate the spread of individual cults. The tradition of this early church was strongly monastic, with groups of clerics living in community. In a more settled age, this produced the *clas* church served by a group of clerics; the characteristic arrangement of such a church may still be seen: an enclosure – the *llan* or the *bangor* – with one or more churches and a number of ancillary buildings. Meifod in Powys is a fine example. Writers of the eleventh and twelfth centuries tended to transfer to earlier centuries the monastic routine with which they were themselves familiar. By the eleventh century the *claswyr* who served in such *clas* churches as Llanddewibrefi, Llanbadarn Fawr and Llancarfan had developed literary traditions of a high order and were practical men of affairs.

Medieval Wales had four dioceses, each with its established cathedral; there are hints that in an earlier age bishops may also have been found in other principal churches. A long succession of bishops can be traced at St David's, the shrine and cathedral associated with St David, the most revered saint in south Wales, and a more limited succession can be traced in the north at Bangor, where St Deiniol had been an important figure. In the south-east, a diocese which extended to the English border was more open to English influence, and so to continental influence, than other Welsh dioceses. Here a succession of bishops can be traced, but the area in which the earliest bishops had oversight and the centre from which they worked cannot easily be defined. By the early years of the twelfth century this diocese was centred on Llandaff, and one of the most fascinating historical problems of early Welsh history is to determine how early this association of diocese and cathedral can be established. The indications are that the early eleventh century is a critical period, but clear definition emerges only in the twelfth century. St Asaph, the fourth diocese in the north-east, is linked with missionary activity at Llanelwy by St Kentigern and his successor, St Asaph. No record of the succession of early bishops survives. A St David's source implies the existence of the diocese in the tenth century, and the name of one bishop consecrated in the eleventh century has been preserved. There is a reference to a diocese in the north-east in the 1120s, but a continuous succession of bishops can only be traced from 1143.

There are few signs that these Welsh dioceses were organized as a recognizable unit, much less as a separate province. St David's preserved the tradition that St David had been both bishop and archbishop. It is clear that the bishops of St David's consecrated new bishops for other sees, and that they had some pre-eminence. From the end of the eleventh century, St David's writers were extending the claims of their diocese. Rhigyfarch, biographer of St David, was either preserving or developing these traditions, which would find stronger and more formal expression from about 1120 to the end of the twelfth century.

There was a strong scholarly tradition, especially in St David's and at Llanbadarn Fawr. Sulien, who held the bishopric of St David's on two occasions (1072–8 and 1080–5), was a scholar trained at Llanbadarn. The details are obscure, but he had also travelled and studied outside Wales and he passed on to another generation the fruits of his learning. His four sons were men of note in the Welsh church; two, Rhigyfarch and Ieuan, left examples of their literary gifts. A third son, Daniel, served as archdeacon of Powys until 1127, and his son was archdeacon of Cardigan until 1163. The skills of another scholarly community at Llancarfan were harnessed for the diocese of Llandaff by Bishop Urban (1107–34).

With the coming of the Normans, men with experience of France and England were appointed to Welsh sees, concepts of morality and of ecclesiastical law acceptable in the European church were introduced, and papal influence became a factor in Welsh ecclesiastical politics. Normans had been active in Wales for more than twenty years before the appointment in 1092 of a Breton, Hervé, as bishop of Bangor. At that stage, Hugh of Chester and Robert of Rhuddlan expected to maintain their tenure of north

Wales, but in the Welsh resurgence of 1094, as the Normans were pushed back beyond the Conwy, Hervé was driven out with them. He spent fifteen years as a querulous exile until Henry I appointed him the first bishop of Ely in 1109. Bangor had no bishop until 1120 when, with Gruffydd ap Cynan in power, David *Scotus* (Scot or, perhaps, Irishman) was appointed.

In Llandaff Herewald, a bishop whose name and connections were English, held the see from 1056 until his death in 1104. Before old age took its toll he had been an effective bishop, modernizing the administration of his diocese. His son, Lifris – in English, Leofric – was a leading figure at the *clas* church at Llancarfan and served him as an archdeacon. For the last twenty years of his life he faced the problems of Norman invasion, despoliation and settlement in his diocese. He was succeeded by another of his archdeacons, Urban (1107–34), who continued to reorganize the see. The church at Llandaff was small, and he replaced it with a large cathedral church. He called on the community of the *clas* church at Llancarfan and used their scholarship and expertise for his diocesan administration. A collection of miscellaneous records relating to the diocese, some of them going back to the late sixth century, exists in the *Book of Llandaff*. The material has been augmented and re-edited in a number of recensions from the ninth century to the early twelfth century, and, with charters recording land transactions especially, to recover the original text has been a long and sometimes contentious process. In the 1120s Urban commissioned what proved to be the final revision of this collection. Our understanding of the *Book of Llandaff* and its value for early Welsh history now depends largely on the studies of Wendy Davies (1982).

The purpose of much of Urban's activity was to define the limits of his diocese and to establish claims to disputed territory. His interest in the *Book of Llandaff* was to use its material to strengthen his claims. At first, Urban called himself bishop of Glamorgan, but by the end of his life he was using the title bishop of Llandaff. He looked west to try to claim churches dedicated to St Teilo, and east to try to reclaim churches dedicated to St Dyfrig. The remarkable thing about him is that he sought judgement in the papal curia and travelled to Rome three times between 1128 and 1134 to argue his case. The decision went against him, but the choice of jurisdiction was important; he may have been a local man, but he saw himself and his diocese in the setting of a European church.

His episcopate was important in another respect. He was consecrated by Archbishop Anselm in 1107, with four English bishops. As a matter of course they made a customary promise of obedience to Anselm as their metropolitan, and Urban gave the same undertaking to the archbishop. The precedent became standard practice for all future Welsh bishops, and the Welsh dioceses were acknowledged to be part of the province of Canterbury. The consequences were far-reaching: a tenuous independence gave way to a formal and, as it proved, unbreakable dependence. For the Anglo-Norman population of the Marches this might make little difference, but for the independent Welsh princes it became a political factor of considerable importance.

Urban became a familiar figure at ecclesiastical councils and at the court of Henry I, and he could turn that to his own advantage. He came to terms with Robert, earl of Gloucester, and they defined their respective rights in the lordship and diocese of Glamorgan. The long document in which this was recorded was issued not in the lordship but at Woodstock, in the presence of Henry I and his court. Urban's privileges had the full sanction of royal authority; against other powerful magnates Urban turned to the papacy for protection.

Llandaff remained closely linked with the lords of Glamorgan, and until the end of the thirteenth century the bishops were either local men or were drawn from no further afield than Hereford or Bristol. William de Saltmarsh, an Augustinian canon from St Augustine's, Bristol, became bishop in 1184, very probably through the patronage of Prince John as lord of the honor of Gloucester and of the lordship of Glamorgan. Gerald of Wales took it for granted that the diocese was in John's gift and claimed that it had been offered to him, though his ambitions lay elsewhere. With two exceptions, there were no long vacancies requiring royal agents to administer the diocese for the benefit of the crown. Royal interest in elections became more obvious from 1230 onwards. The development of diocesan administration, most recently analysed by David Crouch (1988), was a slow process; canons drawn from local Anglo-Norman and Welsh families served the bishops of Llandaff during the twelfth century, and the chapter was formally constituted by Bishop Henry of Abergavenny (1193–1218), with precentor, treasurer, chancellor and two archdeacons.

In west Wales, major changes came with the appointment of a royal official, Bernard, the queen's chancellor, as bishop of St David's in 1115. He used his skills to check Norman encroachments, and to reorganize his diocese. He built up a group of canons at St David's, some from the Welsh clerics already serving the cathedral and others drawn from immigrant families. There was tension between the two groups, which continued long after Bernard's death, but he clearly had the gift of listening to their advice and the sympathy to respond. In 1119 he enhanced the cult of St David by securing from the papacy formal recognition of his canonization. He organized the diocese in archdeaconries and deaneries that reflected traditional territorial divisions; that meant depending heavily on local knowledge. This emerged very strongly in a wider political context. Bernard took up the traditions that Wales should be a separate province with the bishop of St David's as metropolitan. The idea was canvassed at intervals over two decades, and Bernard prepared to submit it formally to the Council of Reims in 1148. He died before the Council met, and the proposal lapsed; whatever the merits of the case, there was nobody to speak boldly in its favour.

The appointment of a local man, David fitz Gerald, as bishop of St David's in 1148 was not dangerous in itself, but it brought together two powerful interests: as a son of Gerald of Windsor he represented an influential marcher family; as the grandson of Rhys ap Tewdwr he represented the ruling dynasty of Deheubarth. After his death in 1176 his nephew Gerald, archdeacon of Brecon, emerged as a potential successor, but on that occasion he was passed over. Peter de Leia, prior of Much Wenlock, was elected, and, like David fitz Gerald before him, he gave an undertaking that he would not raise the question of the metropolitical status of St David's while he was bishop. In the years that followed, Gerald emerged as the leading spokesman for that metropolitical claim and, when he took it up, it was charged with greater political significance.

When the see was vacant again in 1198, Gerald was among those nominated for election, and he believed that Richard I and John would view him favourably and approve his election. He carried his case to the Roman curia, arguing for his own claim as bishop-elect to be consecrated, and for the creation of St David's as an independent archbishopric. He reckoned without Hubert Walter, archbishop of Canterbury, papal legate, and King John's right-hand man in the royal administration. An independent bishop representing local interests and urging separation from Canterbury presented a political threat that Hubert Walter would not countenance. He persuaded John to withdraw his initial approval and he maintained his opposition at the papal curia.

In 1203 Innocent III finally decided against Gerald's claim to be recognized as bishop-elect, and, much weakened by that decision, Gerald accepted defeat on the larger issue of the status of St David's. Gerald was a compulsive writer, and one product of this long conflict was the series of works in which he chronicles his struggle. He was partisan, and in the end embittered; he alienated contemporaries, as he has alienated many of the historians who use his books: but he has provided a wealth of material from which we may try to understand the Welsh church in the second half of the twelfth century.

Innocent's decision was important for the Welsh church, for it established that Wales would not gain the independence that the Irish and Scottish churches had already secured. It also ensured that royal control over the Marches and royal influence elsewhere in Wales would be buttressed by the ecclesiastical discipline which the archbishop of Canterbury could impose. Direct royal influence could be exerted over the nomination and election of bishops for St David's. (Ultimately, the bishop's standing was decided by designating the diocese as a marcher lordship.) Elsewhere, outside the area of Anglo-Norman settlement, a powerful indirect influence could be exerted over the two bishoprics under Welsh control, Bangor and St Asaph. There, in the thirteenth and fourteenth centuries, patriot bishops, committed to the princes of Gwynedd, found themselves with a real, if unwelcome, allegiance to the archbishop of Canterbury.

Norman infiltration into Wales was closely followed by the establishment of monastic houses in their newly acquired lands. In the earliest phase of settlement, the beneficiaries were Benedictine abbeys in France. William fitz Osbern endowed his abbeys of Cormeilles and Lire with churches, lands and tithes and founded the priory of Chepstow as a daughter house of Cormeilles. Further north a Breton, Wihenoc, founded Monmouth Priory and gave it to St Florent of Saumur; Goldcliff was a daughter house of Bec, and Arnulf of Bellême gave Pembroke to the monks of St Martin of Séez. A generation later, English monasteries were given valuable churches and estates in Wales, sometimes as individual grants and, more obviously, as the endowments of a dependent priory. Battle Abbey acquired dependencies at Brecon and Carmarthen, Sherborne Abbey at Kidwelly, Glastonbury at Bassaleg and Tewkesbury at Cardiff. The richest gains were made by St Peter's Abbey at Gloucester, especially in the diocese of Llandaff, dominated as it was by the lords of the honor of Gloucester. The abbey's new wealth included the priory church of Ewenni and its endowments. Such gains were essentially the product of conquest and military occupation, and where that could be challenged endowments could be lost. St Peter's, Gloucester, was given the church of Llanbadarn Fawr as a priory in 1115–16, but that territory could not be held against sustained attack, and the priory was dissolved in 1136. For a brief period the abbey also claimed Cardigan as a dependent priory, but in the confusion of conquest and settlement Cardigan had also been given to the monks of Chertsey, who were able to make good their claims.

The close links between Benedictine monks and settler families remained a permanent feature of the Welsh religious scene. The characteristic Benedictine house was the priory, built under the shadow of a castle, and integrated into the religious and economic life of an Anglo-Norman borough. At Abergavenny the priory church was near the centre of the borough; at Chepstow the priory lay near the castle at the lower end of the little town. The priory at

Brecon was built close to the castle, but beyond the immediate circuit of the borough; even so, it was the parish church for the town and it needed a concession to the burgesses to build a chapel of ease in the centre of the borough. At Kidwelly, castle and priory were separated by the river Gwendraeth, and the priory became a second nucleus for the growth of a community. At Pembroke, too, the priory lay well beyond the town boundary, and the town church enjoyed a separate existence until the advowson was given to the priory. Each case was a variation on a common theme. Recruitment to the Benedictine order was very largely confined to settler families, and the priories were detached from Welsh sentiment and loyalty. Certainly the Black Monks could never create a bridge between the Welsh and the Anglo-Norman settlers.

With the Cistercian order (and the order of Savigny, which joined the Cistercians in 1147) things were very different. Their desire to distance themselves from secular settlements took them in Wales, as elsewhere in Britain, into undeveloped regions. Tintern Abbey, colonized from L'Aumône in 1131, remained essentially an anglicized community and did not establish any daughter house in Wales. In response to an Anglo-Norman patron, Richard de Granville, Savigny sent monks to found Neath Abbey in 1130 in an area with which it had no other connections. A second Welsh house was founded at Basingwerk (normally assigned to 1131), and that should be linked with colonies on the English side of the border at Buildwas and Combermere. Monks from Clairvaux were attracted to south Wales, again by Anglo-Norman patrons. In 1147 Robert, earl of Gloucester, brought them to Margam, a monastery of particular interest for two very different reasons. It received support and endowments from local settler families and from the Welsh dynasties long established in the area, and in the course of time the monks acquired a bad reputation for the ruthless way in which they exploited their arable lands to provide winter pasture for large flocks of sheep.

From Clairvaux, too, came a colony which settled in Dyfed in 1140, establishing their permanent base at Whitland in 1151. They, too, depended upon Anglo-Norman patronage; even in the next generation it was a lord of Norman descent, Robert fitz Stephen, who founded Whitland's daughter house at Strata Florida in 1164. But then a great change occurred. Rhys ap Gruffydd of Deheubarth established control over Strata Florida and Whitland, and, as this family of Cistercian houses grew, it recruited Welshmen as monks and formed strong links with ruling Welsh dynasties. The foundation of new colonies at Strata Marcella (from Whitland, 1170), Aberconwy (from Strata Florida, 1186), Cymer (from Cwmhir, 1198), and Valle Crucis (from Strata Marcella, 1201) created a network of religious houses devoted to independent Welsh sovereignty. The division of monastic allegiance between Anglo-Norman and Welsh was little affected by the foundation of other orders in the twelfth century or, indeed, by foundations of the orders of friars in the thirteenth century. But the impact in terms of literary output and of our understanding of the history of medieval Wales was very profound. Without the Cistercians, the sources for Welsh history in the twelfth and thirteenth centuries would have been overwhelmingly Anglo-Norman, and our view must, inevitably, have been sadly distorted.

4

The Scottish Alliance

In terms of Norman expansion, Scotland is unique. There was never a Norman invasion or conquest. Instead, Anglo–Norman settlers were invited into the kingdom, acquired lordships and fees and established new Anglo–Scottish dynasties. It is not a process that lends itself to any simple catch-phrase; Ritchie (1954) described Scotland as a kingdom that was Norman by adoption, but the phrase did not win approval. It was Normanization undertaken on the initiative of the Scottish kings, and the royal dynasty was itself the principal beneficiary of the whole movement.

The kingdom was in no sense a unity, though the wide prevalence of Gaelic was a unifying factor. There were survivals of Pictish and Irish place-names, language, concepts and traditions. The core of the kingdom lay north of the Firth of Forth, centred on Perth and Scone, the ancient site for the installation and initiation by primitive rites of new kings. The monarchy combined elements drawn from Pictish and Scottish kingship. To the north, the characteristic magnate, in part great lord, in part military commander, was the mormaer, whose jurisdiction may represent ancient areas of Pictish settlement. Six mormaers controlled a range of territories from Strathearn on Tayside, northwards through Angus, Mearns, Mar and Buchan to Moray. They may have been used to defend the northern coastline against Scandinavian attacks.

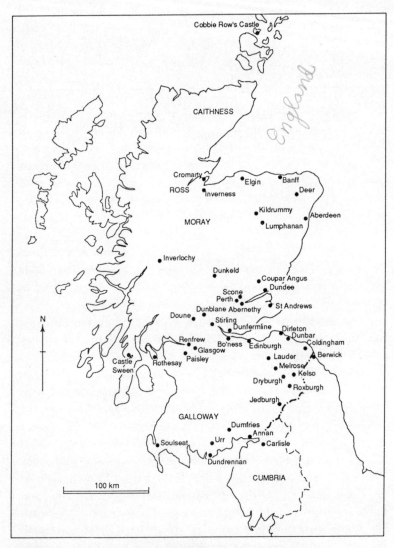

Map 3   Scotland: principal places mentioned in the text

In the twelfth century some of these great lords appear as earls, though it is not always easy to see when the Latin *comes* is used as a technical title or as an equivalent for mormaer. In south-west Scotland the former territory of Strathclyde straddled the Solway Firth and extended from Cumberland and Westmorland to Galloway and Renfrew. Here the dominant influences were Cumbric (Cymric) with close parallels to language and social conditions in Wales. In the south-east, Anglian influences had extended from Northumberland into Lothian, and by contrast Scottish ambitions were to push the Anglo-Scottish frontier beyond the Tweed, with the Tees as a viable and attainable boundary. In the extreme north, along the coastlands of Caithness, in the northern isles of Shetland and Orkney, the western isles of Skye and the Hebrides, the south-western parts of Galloway, and in much of Cumbria, Norwegian settlement was extensive and the earl of Orkney was a power to be reckoned with. Until 1350 his mainland interests were reflected in the formal title earl of Orkney and Caithness.

For some two hundred years, Scottish kingship remained in one dynasty, passing by tanistry to collateral heirs, usually to brother or cousin rather than to son. Three septs within the dynasty contested the crown, and violence and sudden death played a large part in the succession. In 1040 Duncan I, who was campaigning against Moray, was killed by the mormaer Macbeth. By marrying into the royal dynasty Macbeth acquired a veil of legality, while Duncan's sons, Malcolm Canmore and Donald Bàn, both very young boys at the time, found refuge in England. Fourteen years later, with strong English support, Malcolm returned to Scotland and overthrew Macbeth. Even then, three years passed before Macbeth was killed. There was nothing to suggest that these events would mark any change in long-standing custom. But, with one brief interval of conflict, Malcolm Canmore – Malcolm III – and his sons ruled Scotland for ninety-five years. Exactly how strong this hereditary monarchy had become was demonstrated when David I died in 1153. His grandson, Malcolm IV, a boy of twelve, succeeded him. The prospect of a minority was potentially dangerous, but in formal terms there was no minority and in practical terms there was no struggle for power at the royal court. Whoever was then the *éminence grise* cannot be identified – Malcolm's mother Ada de Warenne, Duncan, earl of Fife, Hugh of Morville, the Constable, or one of the Scottish bishops. The most difficult handicap for the young king was that he could not persuade Henry II of England to confer on him the knighthood that would underline the fact that he was his own master. For that Henry made him wait six years. In his later years Malcolm IV was sickly, and perhaps seriously ill; that may be the one factor to explain why he did not marry. When he died in 1165 he was succeeded by his brother William, whose male heirs continued to rule Scotland until 1286. Malcolm III and his sons had achieved a hereditary monarchy on the European pattern, with all the advantages of continuity that could produce.

Throughout this period the Scottish kings were very closely linked with England and English affairs. The hope of controlling Cumberland and Westmorland in the north-west and part (if not all) of Northumbria in the north-east inspired military campaigns and diplomatic initiatives. Malcolm III owed much to the support of his uncle Siward, earl of Northumbria, and to the patronage of Edward the Confessor. When Siward died in 1055 his son Waltheof was passed over in favour of Godwine's son Tostig as earl. The Scots were said to have been quick to test the new earl's strength before he had secured firm control in the north. Malcolm invaded the earldom in 1061, perhaps as an extension of this policy, or perhaps in the interests of the dispossessed Waltheof. It seems to have been an issue of local politics, and that may account for the apparent reversal of policy in 1066 when Malcolm welcomed Tostig, then an exile, and supported the impending Scandinavian invasion of England. In the early years of the Conqueror's reign English dissidents were given refuge in Scotland. Most notably, Edgar the Atheling with his mother and his sisters, Margaret and Christina, were hospitably received. By then, Malcolm's wife Ingibjorg was dead, and he took Margaret as his second wife. Three of their sons were familiar figures at the court of the Anglo-Norman kings and owed much to the patronage of William Rufus and Henry I. Henry himself married one of their daughters, and her sister Mary married the count of Boulogne; in the next generation, Mary's daughter was the wife and queen of King Stephen.

Marriage into the greater Anglo-Norman families increased the links between the Scottish dynasty and English society. In 1122 Alexander I was given Sybil, one of Henry I's illegitimate daughters, in marriage, and despite the bastardy the close link with the English king was intended to be flattering. David, the youngest son, was given Maud of St Liz, daughter and heiress of Earl Waltheof, and her inheritance passed to their successors and not, in the immediate future, to the son of her first marriage. In due course King David's heir, Henry, married Ada de Warenne. In the next generation, King William I's wife was Ermengarde of Beaumont, and his brother David, earl of Huntingdon, married Maud, the daughter of Hugh, earl of Chester.

After David I's marriage, the Scottish king or a near kinsman held the English earldom of Huntingdon. Valuable though that was, it remained a principal ambition to secure recognition as earl of Northumbria with the control of north-east England which that implied, but only in the weakest days of the English monarchy was that achieved. Stephen acknowledged David's son Henry as earl of Northumberland in 1139, and Henry's son William succeeded to that earldom in 1152. But once Henry II was secure on the English throne he abrogated the earlier grant and broke the Scottish connection with Northumberland. Despite these problems the tenure of a large English honor and earldom bound the Scottish dynasty close to the English crown. It also created a network of loyalties and feudal ties between the Scottish kings and their English tenants which would have important consequences for their kingdom.

The earliest Norman influence in Scotland sprang from Lanfranc, archbishop of Canterbury, and his ecclesiastical policy. Source material for the history of the Scottish church in the eleventh and twelfth centuries is both patchy and scarce. Even to record with accuracy the succession of bishops presents acute difficulties; there were long vacancies, and many of the dates suggested for succession are at best tentative. At St Andrews, the succession of bishops between 1028 and 1093 is insecure. There followed a long vacancy before the election in 1107 of Turgot, sometime prior of Durham, and his consecration in 1109. In the past he has been identified, perhaps rather dubiously, as Queen

Margaret's confessor. Further vacancies followed between 1115 and 1123 (with one abortive election) and again from 1159 to 1162. From 1178 a long battle between rival claimants brought weakness to the diocese. Dunblane may have been without a bishop for as long as a century before a regular succession was resumed in or about 1155. At Caithness there is no evidence of any bishop holding the see before the reign of King David I. From the 1050s to the 1120s the diocese of Glasgow was closely associated with York, and bishops of Glasgow appear as suffragan bishops in northern England; in their absence, the cathedral, and probably the diocese, may have been left without episcopal oversight for more than seventy years (Duncan, 1975). A few personal names, unmistakably Scottish, point to an active native episcopate: Cormac of Dunkeld in the 1120s, Gilla-Aldan of Whithorn (1128), Nechtan of Aberdeen (1132), Macbeth of Ross in the 1130s and Andrew of Caithness (1128). Macbeth's successors at Ross, Simon and Gregory, have been identified tentatively as the last in a line of Scottish bishops in the north (Duncan, 1975). A little later, Ragnald, bishop of the Isles (*c*.1166–*c*.1170), was clearly a man drawn from local Scandinavian stock.

Bishops appointed in the reigns of David I, Malcolm IV and William I were often men of immigrant stock serving under royal patronage, and by 1214, if not considerably earlier, they were fully integrated into the Anglo-Scottish society of the Lowlands. John, bishop of Glasgow, consecrated some time between 1114 and 1118, had served David I as chaplain when he was still earl of Huntingdon and lord of Cumbria. Edward, bishop of Aberdeen (1151), was David I's chancellor; Walter de Bidun, who was elected bishop of Dunkeld in 1178 but never consecrated, was chancellor under David I and his two grandsons. Ingram of Glasgow (1164) was also chancellor under Malcolm IV. There was clearly a large-scale movement from native Scottish to immigrant bishops, whether they are to be described as Norman, Anglo-Norman or Anglo-Scottish.

Little is known of the consecration of Scottish bishops, even in the twelfth century. St Andrews enjoyed a tradition of primacy, but the assumption is normally made that a newly elected Scottish bishop was consecrated by his fellow-bishops without reference to a *primus inter pares* or to a metropolitan. In 1072, when he had forced the archbishop of York, Thomas of Bayeux, into temporary submission, Lanfranc acknowledged York's claims to have over-sight of the Scottish church. As late as 1165 the papacy formally accepted the Scottish bishops as dependencies of York, though in practice antipathy to York's claims grew steadily as the twelfth century advanced. Turgot, bishop of St Andrews (1109), and Michael, nominated to Glasgow by the king's brother David (be-tween 1109 and 1114), were consecrated by the archbishop of York and gave him the promise of obedience due to a metropolitan. Robert, elected to St Andrews in 1123, was eventually consecrated by Archbishop Thurstan of York in 1127, but he refused to make any promise of obedience. The position was made more confusing because archbishops of York consecrated a number of bishops of the Isles and Orkney to serve as suffragan bishops in the diocese of York.

At the beginning of the twelfth century Glasgow was in a similar position, but there the bishops gradually escaped from English control. Some time between 1114 and 1118 Bishop John was con-secrated by Pope Pascal II, and York's claims were then ignored. When Herbert, abbot of Kelso, was elected to Glasgow in 1147 the diocese of York was vacant, and he went for consecration to Eugenius III at Auxerre. In 1164, Ingram followed his example and went to Sens to be consecrated by Alexander III; eleven years later Jocelin, abbot of Melrose, went to Clairvaux for consecration by a papal legate. Alexander III played a very significant role in the process. Twice he issued bulls giving Glasgow his special protec-tion, defining the diocese in unequivocal terms as a special daugh-ter with no intermediary between pope and bishop.

Much of this must be linked with English policy and with re-lations between England and the papacy, deeply affected by Henry II's quarrel with Becket and by the consequences of the arch-bishop's murder. King Henry sought to make political capital from the capture of the Scottish king, William the Lion – William I – in 1174. As part of the conditions for his release William had to promise the subjection of the Scottish church to the English church, and a year later a number of Scottish bishops and abbots were obliged to give their fealty to Henry II. At the council of Northampton in 1176 Henry drove the Scots harder, demanding the obedience due from all the Scottish bishops, but they were able to turn the challenge to their own advantage. By way of answer they could produce the clear evidence of the long independence of the diocese of Glasgow, and the king's ambitions were checked. In 1176 a papal legate arrived in Scotland, beyond Henry's reach, and denounced the oath of obedience demanded from the Scottish bishops. So, on papal authority, the archbishop of York was forbidden to intervene in Scotland. The full formal recognition of the independence of the Scottish church came in 1192, but by then that independence had been acknowledged in practice for sixteen years. The long sequence of events springing from Lanfranc's intervention and from York's pursuit of metropolitical authority in Scotland had ended in failure. Success for the Scottish kingdom had been won by a dynasty more Anglo-Norman than Scottish, served by an episcopate that was itself largely Anglo-Norman. Only in one sense was their success qualified rather than total: although the Scottish church was an independent province it had to wait until 1472 before the first Scottish archbishopric was established at St Andrews, and until 1492 for a second archiepiscopal see to be established at Glasgow.

While political events can be discerned clearly, personal influence is much harder to identify and assess. This is particularly marked in Scotland with the influence attributed to Queen Margaret. Her marriage to Malcolm Canmore is properly regarded as the introduction of religious and cultural changes in Scotland, though in recent studies her influence has been questioned if not diminished. The new queen was deeply religious; her piety and devotion had been formed in exile in Hungary and owed much to the influence of the orthodox church. She had a natural liking for children and she had close bonds with, and strong influence over, her own family. There are clear indications that Malcolm was an indulgent husband. None of their children was given a Scottish name; instead, their English names reflect their mother's pride in her own ancestry. It is curious that Malcolm did not seek to ensure

Scottish loyalty by giving even one of their sons a name reflecting similar pride in their Scottish ancestry. Does it, perhaps, imply that he thought the succession to be secure in his son Duncan, and that Margaret's children were not likely to be politically significant? It could be said that Margaret's strongest influence was in the training of her younger children for the royal authority which, unexpectedly, they would one day exercise.

In practical terms, Margaret acted in rather surprising fashion. She demonstrated a strong veneration, not for saints with whom she was familiar in her youth, but for St Andrew and the cult centred on the cathedral complex at St Andrews. She also showed a deep sympathy for the holy men of the old Scottish church, defined sometimes as hermits and in other contexts as Culdees. She wrote to Archbishop Lanfranc seeking his advice, and he replied in a fulsome, almost obsequious letter. She and her husband were described in flattering terms, but it may be that there was a genuine admiration and perhaps an early recognition of her reputation in the phrase the archbishop used to describe her: a 'queen beloved of God'. The outcome of their exchange of letters was that Lanfranc sent three monks from Canterbury to establish a Benedictine community at Dunfermline. Apart from her patronage of Dunfermline the queen's achievements were limited. She gave her support to St Andrews and enhanced the cathedral church, and for the benefit of pilgrims she established a ferry across the Firth of Forth, Queensferry. For the most part she was a woman who lived through her children, and her influence can best be seen in their support for the church in later years.

The main feature of Scottish history in the twelfth century was the influx of foreign settlers drawn from England, Normandy, Brittany and Flanders, which it is convenient to describe as Anglo-Norman. The analysis of this process has been dominated over the past forty years by Geoffrey Barrow. Themes which he first formulated in early papers and in *Feudal Britain* (1956) have been explored in depth in his introductory essays to the first two volumes of *Regesta Regum Scottorum* (Barrow, 1960; Barrow and Scott, 1971) and given full expression in *The Anglo-Norman Era in Scottish History* (1980).

The first important question is to ask how early this settlement can be established. While Malcolm III reigned, English refugees of noble birth found a safe haven in Scotland. Queen Margaret was attended by two English ladies, and with her brother and sister they were a small group of exiles at the royal court. Edgar the Atheling was given honourable status; much later, in the 1070s, he was provided with men and arms on a generous scale for his interventions in Norman politics, but he did not become a great landowner in Scotland. Cospatric, exiled earl of Northumbria, was the son of a Scottish father and an English mother, and he was King Malcolm's first cousin. He fled from England, and when the king gave him the land that formed the core of the earldom of Dunbar he was providing for a close kinsman. Cospatric's dynasty survived for eight generations before the direct male line failed and their inheritance passed to a collateral branch. Two English nobles, Marleswein and Archill, found permanent homes in Scotland and may have been given land by Malcolm III.

A Marleswein son of Colban held land at Kennoway; about 1160 he gave property there to St Andrews but he was in part confirming a grant made by an earlier Marleswein, who was presumably the English fugitive. The family was still acquiring new estates in the reign of William the Lion. After Malcolm's death in 1093, Donald Bàn gained support from those who resented the foreign settlers who had enjoyed the late king's favour; that may perhaps indicate settlement on a larger scale than the sources record.

In terms of immigration, Malcolm's reign can be regarded with some justification as a clearly defined episode. Movement across the frontier was confined to English refugees. He was no friend of the Norman kings, nor of Anglo-Norman magnates. He mounted a savage campaign in Northumbria in 1070. That and his marriage into the royal dynasty of Ethelred II prompted the Conqueror to lead a combined land and naval force to Scotland in 1072; this penetrated north of the Forth into the heartland of Malcolm's kingdom. At Abernethy the two kings made peace: Malcolm did homage, acknowledged King William's lordship and gave hostages, including his own son Duncan. In 1079, and again in 1091, Malcolm invaded Northumbria. The first attack was followed by a long period of peace, but the second led to further discord. William Rufus made terms which were not fulfilled to Malcolm's satisfaction. In 1093, guaranteed safe conduct so that he could travel south to settle these issues with William Rufus, he arrived at Gloucester, but Rufus refused to meet him. Humiliated and rebuffed, he returned to Scotland and mounted another raid on Northumbria, but as he moved north towards the border he was intercepted at Alnwick and there he and his son Edward were killed. It was the end of a long and influential reign, and the note of finality was reinforced by the death of Queen Margaret four days later.

With the succession of his son, Edgar, we are on the verge of a new era in Scottish history, the era of Anglo-Norman immigration. Donald Bàn's attempt to secure the throne in the years 1093–7 meant that Edgar and his brothers had to find refuge in England, and it was with help from William Rufus that Edgar was eventually established king. From 1094, right through the twelfth century, English patronage and English lordship were major influences. To see Anglo-Norman immigration in perspective it is useful to move forward to 1174, and to identify what has happened over a period of eighty years: then some of the details of when and how it occurred can be examined and assessed. The early years of the reign of William the Lion, from his accession at the end of 1165 to his capture in July 1174, form a compact and illuminating period. Using those of his charters for which witness lists have survived, his *acta* were attested by 115 men clearly of Anglo-Norman provenance, and at the most by twenty-five men clearly of Scottish stock. That alone points to a remarkable change in the structure of Scottish society over some eighty years. The greater part of the immigration which produced that change took place in the reigns of David I and Malcolm IV, and it was still in progress in William's reign. How far back does it go?

For Edgar's reign – he was securely established in Scotland from 1097 to 1107 – the evidence of English or Anglo-Norman infiltration is so slight that firm conclusions are scarcely justified (cf. Duncan, 1975). The general form of address used in Edgar's writs was to all his men, Scots and English. The text of one crucial charter issued in 1095 has survived. It was issued at Norham in

Northumberland, and the names of the witnesses who were in the king's entourage have been preserved in mangled form. They include Scottish and Northumbrian names. There is one Anglo-Norman name, Robert de Homet, an early representative of the family of du Hommet, which was holding land in Yorkshire by the first decade of the twelfth century. One knight who served Edgar can be identified by name: Robert, son of Godwine; he was given land in Lothian and, despite his name, half French, half English, he set about building a castle (no doubt a motte) there. He was a man trained in continental practices. At best, we have indications that movements were taking place across the frontier and a hint that the potential immigrants would not all be of English stock.

There are similar indications that under Alexander I Anglo-Norman influences continued and perhaps developed. He was responsible for early work on Stirling castle, and either he or his predecessor must have been responsible for the early twelfth-century work at the castle of Edinburgh. He is said to have given land to settlers who would carry out military duties. A Frenchman, Robert of Burgundy, held land in Lochore in 1112–16 and had been settled long enough to burden the Culdees of St Serf's island in Loch Leven with his demands, for which he was brought to justice. How long the community suffered before seeking redress is a matter of surmise, but Robert's tenure may date from Alexander's reign. The king used the services of an envoy who could be described as a knight.

In administration external influences may also be discerned. The name of the first chancellor to serve the Scottish kings, Herbert, appeared in the later years of the reign; he continued to serve David I until 1131. It is also abundantly clear that Alexander was open to English influence in ecclesiastical affairs. Turgot of Durham was elected bishop of St Andrews in 1107, and again in 1120 Alexander drew another English monk, Eadmer of Canterbury, as bishop-elect of St Andrews, though he was never consecrated. Of more lasting importance was the recruitment of six canons from the Augustinian priory at Nostell to establish a priory at Scone.

The critical feature of Alexander I's reign was the position accorded to his brother David. Land from Strathclyde to Teviotdale was given to him, a legacy, as it was said to be, from King Edgar.

Alexander was able to delay the transfer of this valuable land for six years, but in 1113 David could introduce new men and new ideas from his English estates. It is no accident that judges occur as significant local figures in Nithsdale and Cumbria before the end of the reign. The king was certainly affected by English influences, but the real initiative lay with his younger brother.

With the accession of David as king in 1124 the pace changed, and Anglo-Norman families settled in Scotland in large numbers. The explanation lies very largely in David's long apprenticeship before he became king. The succession of three sons of Malcolm III and Margaret within thirty years (*c.*1095–1124) obscures the fact that younger brothers naturally assumed they would never be serious contenders for the crown. Since Edgar was unmarried, Alexander was his obvious heir, and the king gave him a considerable territory in Scotland. David, as the youngest brother, was not at that stage a likely candidate for the throne, and when in 1100 his sister married Henry I David joined her entourage, seeking fortune under Henry's patronage. His reward came through his marriage, about 1114, to Maud of St Liz, with her honor and the earldom of Huntingdon.

Living in England from 1100 until his accession in 1124, David acquired a wide circle of friends and dependants in Anglo-Norman society. His place in Henry I's court brought him into close contact with a group of men from Henry's lordship in western Normandy (Barrow, 1980): Robert de Brus from Brix, Hugh of Morville, Ranulph de Soules, from Soulles, and Robert Avenel, whose family held land further south in the Avranchin. The knightly tenants of the earldom of Huntingdon, settled mostly in the shires of Huntingdon and Northampton, served him as their lord, and many of them joined him later in Scotland. These were not mutually exclusive groups. David was responsible for enfeoffing Hugh of Morville and Ranulph de Soules in his earldom some time after 1124; Robert de Brus was lord of Cleveland in the north-east, and before 1124 he frequently travelled around with David and attested charters that he was issuing as earl of Huntingdon.

From the beginning of his reign, David was creating enfeoffments – infeftments is the accurate term in Scottish law – in southern Scotland, perhaps formalizing arrangements that had been made in the last ten years of his brother's reign. Robert de Brus held Annandale (probably for the service of ten knights), and his tenure was recorded as early as 1124. To the east, the Avenels would be found in Eskdale, and the de Soules in Liddesdale. To the north of their territories, Hugh of Morville held a compact lordship in Cunningham; elsewhere he also held a lordship in the eastern Lowlands at Lauderdale. From the borders of Normandy and Brittany, Henry I had drawn into his service the hereditary seneschal of the bishops of Dol, Alan, son of Flaad. Endowed with estates in England, he was the ancestor of the fitz Alans, lords of Oswestry and later of Arundel. His youngest son Walter was established in Scotland by about 1136 and was given extensive lands along the Firth of Clyde. One lordship was made up of Renfrew and Mearns and the estates attached to them, together with a stretch of wilder country in the valley of the river Gryfe and the moorlands lying between the river and the west coast. To these were added the lands in Ayrshire later identified as Kyle Stewart, while elsewhere in Scotland Malcolm IV gave Walter land in Roxburghshire, East Lothian and Berwickshire. One substantial lordship bordering the greater native lordship of Galloway was Nithsdale, which King David left in the hands of a local dynasty. The southern part of this territory was reclaimed by the crown in the 1160s, and the castle of Dumfries had been built by the king well before 1177.

Three families owed much to their tenure of hereditary offices. Hugh of Morville was David I's constable as early as 1140, and the office remained with his heirs until the failure of the male line in 1196. Ranulph de Soules was identified as the king's butler as early as the reign of Malcolm IV and had probably been given the office by David I. There was a break in their tenure of this office during the reign of William the Lion, but by the early thirteenth century it had been re-established as a hereditary office in the de Soules family. Walter, son of Alan, was appointed steward by King David and held the office until his death in 1177; it passed to his heirs and, in due course, became their dynastic name (comparable to the Butlers of Ireland). Patronage meant opportunity and wealth, and these hereditary office holders were well placed to build up their possessions in Scotland.

David I was also concerned to establish in Scotland men of more limited means; he granted land to a number to hold directly of the crown for the service of a single knight. Some of them were settled in the less dangerous areas of the Scottish Lowlands.

This process of settlement was maintained throughout the reigns of Malcolm IV and William the Lion, and it can be seen at a slower pace in the thirteenth century. It attracted new men from many parts of England. The greater number were drawn from Huntingdonshire and Northamptonshire; immigrants from Yorkshire and Northumbria can be traced from the beginning of David I's reign to the middle of the thirteenth century. A number of families were recruited from Devon, Somerset and the south-west.

As with so much of Norman expansion, those who were attracted to Scotland were predominantly younger sons whose landed endowment in France or England would of necessity be small. Walter, son of Alan, was the youngest of three brothers, each of them having land and influence in a different country, one in Brittany, another in England, Walter himself in Scotland. A fortuitous marriage with the daughter of King Robert I and the failure of Bruce heirs brought the Stewarts to the throne in 1371. Different branches of the same family could have interests on different sides of the Anglo-Scottish frontier. Barrow (1980) has traced one such family, the de Vaux, which settled in northern England and southern Scotland. Robert, from the English branch, founded an Augustinian priory at Lanercost between 1165 and 1169; from the Scottish branch, a generation later, John de Vaux was a benefactor of the priory. The origins of both branches lie in an estate near Rouen where the family can be identified in the middle years of the twelfth century. But how the two branches divided and sought new lands beyond Normandy is entirely a matter of surmise.

It seems clear that the consolidation of holdings, the definition of military service and the building of castles were all prominent features of the reign of William the Lion. Many ringworks and more than 240 mottes have been identified; many more sites need further investigation. A large number of these must be associated with the extension of royal authority, and of the Anglo-Norman settlement that accompanied it, during and after William's reign. The independence of Fergus, lord of Galloway, who claimed quasi-royal standing in his territories until his eclipse in 1160, was maintained in large measure by his sons. A network of castles was built to contain this dynasty and gradually to bring their territory under subjection. From the lordship of Annandale to the western coast of Galloway, some sixty-five castle sites still survive. If one castle had to be singled out for special mention it could well be the motte established by Walter de Berkeley at Urr, the largest motte in Scotland. With so many castles in this area, it has been compared to the marchlands of Wales, where the heavy concentration of castles was made necessary by the turbulent conditions of the marches.

Royal expansion in this south-western part of Scotland was not easily achieved. The royal castle at Dumfries was taken and destroyed, probably in 1174; its loss was part of the temporary eclipse of royal power in the area which followed the capture of William the Lion by English forces. It was a mark of the resilience of the Scottish dynasty and its supporters that the construction of a new castle was begun in 1179; that opened a new phase in a long process, and castle-building and containment were to be a characteristic of the next fifty years. In two successive generations between 1160 and 1185 the control of Galloway was disputed by the sons and grandsons of Fergus. In the 1190s a family agreement left one grandson Lachlan as lord of Galloway, and his rival Duncan as lord of Carrick. Lachlan, who also used the name Roland, married the heiress of the Morville lordships and in 1196 assumed control of her lands. Their son Alan was a man of great power, whose influence extended far beyond Galloway. In 1210 King John saw him as a useful ally in Ulster and gave him a large holding of 140 knights' fees to secure his support. The Scottish kings could maintain their pressure on Galloway well into the thirteenth century, but they could not subdue it.

In northern and western Scotland families of ancient lineage were powerful. The earldoms of Atholl, Angus and Buchan remained in the hands of Scottish dynasties, though they were brought under royal surveillance. Moray posed a greater threat; there the Mac Heth mormaers had close links of kinship with the ruling dynasty, and between 1130 and 1142 their kinsmen produced two dangerous claimants to the Scottish throne. David I countered this threat from the north by encouraging immigrants to settle in eastern Moray. To Freskin, a Fleming already settled in the lordship of Strathbrock, south of the Forth, he gave a large stretch of territory near Elgin based on Duffus, where he built a motte.

In the next generation, Berowald, another Flemish settler established in Lothian, was given land in the province of Elgin at Innes and Nether Urquhart. A Flemish plantation, organized by immigrants already familiar with Lowland Scotland, was clearly part of the royal encroachment on Moray. Before 1214 royal castles had been established at Elgin, Forres, Auldearn and Inverness, and probably at three other sites, and with each castle a royal burgh developed. Behind the exposed outposts along the coast of the Moray Firth could be found an increasing number of castles. There were three important mottes in Aberdeenshire: the Doune of Invernochty, which may have been built before 1183; Inverurie, which was established before 1214; and the Peel of Lumphanan, which was built between 1222 and 1228. The western parts of Moray were gradually brought under control in the reigns of William the Lion and Alexander II, with further immigration by men already settled in Scotland as part of that process. The whole area was protected by at least fifty, and perhaps as many as eighty, ringworks and mottes.

The expansion of royal control to the northernmost parts of Scotland was achieved gradually, again through the intensive use of castles, and was marked by violence and hostility. Perhaps the clearest indication of a new regime at work in the north is to be found in the creation of the earldom of Sutherland. The succession of earls from 1214 onwards shows no sign of ancient Scottish lineage. The neighbouring earldom of Ross shows a significant change with the death of Malcolm Mac Heth in 1168. He was not followed by any of his own kinsmen, and in the thirteenth century the succession of earls no longer represented separatist interests. In his account of these events, A. A. M. Duncan (1975) quotes the comment of an Augustinian writing at Barnwell, in Cambridgeshire, 'the more recent kings of the Scots . . . profess themselves to be rather Frenchmen in race, manners, language and outlook; and after reducing the Scots to utter servitude they admit only Frenchmen to their friendship and service.' In the early thirteenth century, this was already a very conservative, not to say archaic, comment on the monarchy, but it reflects the deep resentment of the men of Ross and Caithness as they were brought directly under the control of kings whose power base lay in southern and central Scotland.

There was a similar extension of royal authority in western Scotland. As the power of the rulers of the western Isles declined Walter, son of Alan, could move from the mainland along the Firth of Clyde onto the island of Bute, with Rothesay as his principal base. He may have gained a foothold in the island as early as 1164, and his castle is thought to have been established well before 1200.

Those who settled in Scotland were immigrants who merged into Scottish society, some as an aristocratic elite, some as members of a burghal society, some as tillers of the soil. They did not come as conquerors, though the part they played in the expansion of royal power may demand subtle redefinition of that claim. In the light of recent interpretations of Norman settlements (see pp. 21–3) they may be regarded as colonists, deliberately called in to a new country to develop and exploit its resources. They did so, not in the interest of an external power, but in the interest of the ruling dynasty. Gradually they were absorbed into Scottish society.

The fusion may be explained in three ways. First, in Scotland, as in Ireland, familiar names were altered subtly into names that were recognizably Scottish. Second, in at least a dozen earldoms the ancient lines of Scottish magnates continued unchanged, and dynasties that were already established in the twelfth century were maintained, though not always through direct male descent, throughout the medieval period. There is nothing to compare with the displacement of Welsh and Irish dynasties or with the humiliation of even their strongest rulers.

The third reason deserves closer attention. It is that there does not appear to be a sharp division between the use of patronage by the monarchy and the aristocracy. David I himself was unconventional in his choice of the order of Tiron as a source for his own foundation at Selkirk (1113), which was transferred to Kelso in 1128, and for Lesmahagow (1144). The Cistercians found him a generous patron with the foundation of Melrose Abbey (1136), Newbattle (1140) and Kinloss (1150). He established Augustinian houses at Holy Rood, Edinburgh (1128), Jedburgh (1138–9), and outside Stirling the community which became known as Cambuskenneth (before 1147). Malcolm IV established Cistercians at Coupar Angus between 1161 and 1164, and Augustinians at Restenneth, again in Angus, in 1162. Old-established magnates and newcomers alike encouraged new foundations. Fergus of Galloway brought the Cistercians to Dundrennan in 1142, and Premon-stratensians to Soulseat a decade later. Hugh of Morville founded one of the great centres of monastic life in southern Scotland when he, too, established English canons of the order of Prémontré at Dryburgh, a house formally recognized in 1152. When William, son of Alan, founded a Cluniac monastery at Paisley, he was much influenced by his earlier experience of Cluniacs at Much Wenlock in Shropshire. At a later date a new generation of magnates spon-sored foundations. Members of the royal family established Tironian monks at Lindores and Cistercians at Balmerino, and northern earls recruited Cistercians from Kinloss for their foun-dations at Culross and Deer. These examples all suggest a common enterprise, free of any political or emotional overtones due to race or allegiance.

5

The Irish Intransigence

The Norman incursions and settlements in Ireland present a case history of particular fascination. In the first place, the earliest contingents arrived in Leinster in 1169, a century after the Norman invasion of England, and in that long period Ireland had responded to continental influences, especially in terms of the Irish church. Where, in England and Wales, invaders from Normandy had found much that was strange and unfamiliar, in Ireland invaders from south Wales found much that was familiar and easy to take for granted. A second and very important feature is that 'Norman' is no longer a satisfactory term to describe these adventurers (Davies, 1990). After a century of settlement in England and Wales they are better described as Anglo–Norman, though that may not do justice to the strong Welsh element in the Norman families from south Wales, which played a major role in Ireland.

In the eleventh century the long-standing isolation of the Irish church was checked, and increasing exposure to the influence of the European church brought about important changes. Irish monks and scholars were familiar figures in Germany and had close connections with monasteries at Ratisbon, Würzburg and Mainz. As early as 1028 Sitric, the Norse king of Dublin, and Flanducan, king of the neighbouring territory of Bregia, went on pilgrimage to Rome. Some forty years later Donnchad, son of Brian Bóruma, journeyed to Rome and died on his pilgrimage in 1064. A decade

Map 4   Ireland: principal places mentioned in the text

later Pope Gregory VII wrote to his successor Turlough O'Brien, and thereafter the papacy could exercise a stronger influence over the Irish church (Watt, 1970, 1972).

For practical purposes, links with England were more significant. Soon after 1028, under Sitric's patronage, Dunan, first bishop of Dublin, was consecrated, probably at Canterbury. Political links between the Scandinavians of south-east Ireland and the powerful dynasty of the earls of Mercia, and commercial links with Bristol, in the reign of Edward the Confessor, strengthened the connection. When the bishopric became vacant in 1074, these links reinforced earlier ties and the men of Dublin sent their new bishop, Patrick, to be consecrated by Lanfranc at Canterbury. Patrick, in turn, sent his future successor, Donngus (1085–96), to be a monk at Canterbury in preparation for his future work. Following the same pattern, Donngus sent his nephew Samuel to be a monk at St Albans, to be trained as his successor. In 1096 Archbishop Anselm consecrated the first bishop of Waterford, Máel Ísu Ua hAinmere – Malchus or Malachy. All these were Irish ecclesiastics whose connections with the archbishop of Canterbury and with English monastic foundations could be seen as sources of strength. There was a price to pay, for these bishops accepted the archbishop of Canterbury as their metropolitan. Lanfranc asserted his claim to authority over the Irish church, but it was the consecration of Patrick that gave him the chance to exercise his influence in a very limited sphere. He could send the new bishop back to Dublin with letters for Guthric, king of Dublin, and Turlough O'Brien, king of Munster, urging reform of the lax marriage customs which prevailed in Ireland. In 1080 or 1081 he was consulted by Domnall, bishop of Killaloe, and other clerics, who asked him to resolve a theological issue: were baptized children who died before they had received the body and blood of Christ lost in eternity? With his usual methodical scholarship, he made it clear that baptism alone was essential. They also sent him problems of 'profane learning', but Lanfranc declared that he had long since given up such studies, and he would not be drawn.

Archbishop Anselm maintained the contact and wrote to the Irish bishops as a group, not insisting upon a theoretical claim but clearly identifying himself as their arbiter if they should find problems they could not resolve. In his dealings with Murchetach O'Brien and the bishops of Dublin, Waterford and Limerick, he used careful but unmistakable language of authority.

Canterbury's primacy was never accepted by the whole Irish church. Armagh was consistently a centre of resistance. In 1121 Gregory, bishop-elect of Dublin, asked Ralph d'Escures, then archbishop of Canterbury, to consecrate him and he explained that there was jealousy and tension between Dublin and Armagh. He declared that the bishops of Dublin wished always to be subject to Canterbury. Ironically, thirty-one years later Gregory became the first archbishop of Dublin and the link with Canterbury was severed.

Perhaps the chief reason for this was the increasing influence of the papacy in the Irish church. When Gregory VII wrote to Turlough O'Brien, he wrote in general and courteous terms; specific criticism of Irish customs could follow. His letter served to establish direct papal concern for the Irish church, a concern that was later to find expression through the appointment of papal legates in Ireland. The reform of the Irish church in the twelfth century was achieved largely through a series of councils over which papal legates presided, held between 1101 and 1217. In 1101 the ruling king of Munster, Murchetach O'Brien, handed over to the church the ancient royal stronghold and residence at Cashel, and the occasion was marked by a council under the presidency of the legate, Bishop Máel Muire O'Doonan. A decade later, at the council of Rathbreasil, Gilbert, bishop of Limerick, introduced the first stage of a reform of the Irish episcopate. Gilbert was probably a Norman; he had links with Rouen and had come into contact with Anselm both as abbot of Bec and as archbishop of Canterbury. His affiliations were with Europe rather than with England. Gilbert, who was responsible for a study of the European church and its hierarchy, which may have been influential in Ireland, was legate for twenty-eight years.

The problem tackled and partly solved at Rathbreasil was that of the instability of the Irish episcopate. Archbishops were appointed at Armagh and Cashel, and an attempt was made to establish

permanent bishoprics. A similar exercise was carried out in 1152 at
the council which met partly at Kells (Meath) and partly at
Mellifont, when Dublin and Tuam were also created arch-
bishoprics, each with its suffragan bishoprics carefully defined.
What in earlier centuries had been a church dominated by monastic foundations was transformed into a church controlled by its
bishops. In the early stages of this process some pressure was
brought to bear, and some influence exerted, from Canterbury, but
overall the stronger influence came from the papacy.

Until 1169 the Irish church responded to these reforming influences, but it developed without violent change. There were some
4,000 sites hallowed by different associations: holy wells, early
crosses, monastic foundations or ancient churches, long usage
as burial grounds and, above all, links with early Celtic saints.
Few sites retain the sharp definition of the boundaries, or the
rich evidence of continuity of occupation, of Clonmacnois or
Glendalough. Well-defined boundary embankments, like those at
Rahan, Kilfenora and Kilvoyden, can best be appreciated from
aerial photographs. Many of these sites combined monastic foundations with secular settlements; they were densely populated, and
it is possible to speak of them as having 'some kind of urban
character', or to regard a site such as Glendalough or the centre of
the cult of St Patrick at Armagh as a 'proto-town'.

In the principal foundations it is common to find a number of
churches in use. Small stone churches with corbelled roofs have
been assigned to various periods from the ninth century to the
twelfth. In a simple and early form the style is to be found in
Gallarus's oratory on the Dingle peninsula. It was essentially a
technique which produced buildings capable of remaining effective
for many centuries, and often a particular building must be dated
provisionally by the details of its decoration. Wooden churches
were replaced by stone churches, and in Ireland as in Anglo-Saxon
England the stone church was built in close imitation of the
earlier wooden structure. With these archaic forms, Romanesque
churches appeared in Ireland long before the advent of the
Normans. Cormac's chapel at Cashel, built between 1127 and 1134,
is the Romanesque church from which much of the inspiration for

the new style sprang. (These developments are discussed in chapter 6.)

In the first half of the twelfth century new monastic foundations appeared in Ireland. They were the product of European, but not of Norman, influence. Tentative efforts to establish the Benedictines met with very little success. A kinsman of the king of Desmond, Cormac Mac Carthy, was a monk at Regensburg, and at some time between 1121 and 1133 the abbot of Regensburg sent two Irish monks and two craftsmen to Cashel, where a priory was established. Two Savigniac abbeys were founded at Erenagh in 1127 and at Dublin in 1139. Technically Benedictine, they were much influenced by the Cistercians and they formally joined the Cistercian order in 1147. A small number of Benedictine houses were later established under Norman patronage.

The future was to lie with the Cistercians and the Augustinians. The leading figure in this renewed monastic life was a product of the old Irish tradition, Máel Máedóc Ua Morgair, St Malachy, monk, abbot and bishop. His training and his ideals he gained at Armagh. He was particularly influential as bishop of Down (1124–32 and 1136–48) and briefly as archbishop of Armagh (1132–6). Throughout his life he was in touch with monastic houses and leaders beyond the borders of Ireland. He was believed to have visited the Savigniac monastery at Tulketh in Lancashire in about 1126 and the house of Augustinian canons at Guisborough in Yorkshire at some date before 1137. In 1139–40 he visited Rome, where he was appointed papal legate, and he spent some time at Clairvaux with the friend and admirer who became his biographer, St Bernard. He also visited Arrouaise, in the diocese of Amiens, an Augustinian house where the observances of the community were strongly influenced by Cistercian practice. There he had the rule and observances copied so that he could take them back to Ireland.

The results of his patronage could be seen on a large scale by the time of his death in 1148. When Erenagh was founded in 1127 it was understood to have enjoyed his approval, even if his initiative cannot be established. As legate, from 1140 until his death in 1148, he introduced and encouraged Augustinian monasteries. At least twenty Arrouaisian houses were established under his direct influence, and he may have been responsible for another fourteen for which the foundation dates are less secure. His most important initiative was to found in 1142 the Cistercian monastery at Mellifont; this was to become the parent monastery of a family of Cistercian colonies. Before Malachy's death, daughter houses had been established at Baltinglass, Bective, Boyle, Monasteranenagh and Suir. The full range of monastic foundations which, in England, would be regarded as a consequence of the Norman conquest, was in Ireland due to the initiative and patronage of Irish churchmen and, pre-eminently, of Malachy himself.

It need not be a cause for surprise that an examination of the Norman impact on Ireland should require so detailed a survey of events and movements that had made their mark before any adventurer from the Anglo-Norman kingdom had set foot in Ireland. Nor should it cause surprise that it will be necessary to select examples from the mass of detailed information available about many of the sorties and campaigns that marked the Norman advances in Ireland after 1169.

The intrusion of the Anglo-Norman adventurers in Ireland was the product of conflict between Irish dynasties. Overall, the high king (the *ardri*) could claim and sometimes exercise authority over a large part of the island (Binchy, 1970; Byrne, 1973). The role of the high king seemed to be given sharper definition by Brian Bóruma, king of Munster, whose dominance was widely recognized from 1002 until his death in 1014. His son and successor, Donnchad, retained the high kingship over a long reign until he was overthrown in 1064. Thereafter, three dynasties contested the high kingship: the O'Briens of Munster; the Mac Loughlins, a sept of the O'Neills established in Tyrone which assumed its own patronymic *c*.1024; the O'Connors of Connacht. The clear indication that the high kings were no longer dominant is that they could be described as kings 'facing opposition'. Their authority depended upon regular supremacy in warfare or upon a shifting pattern of alliances with client kings of lesser stature. So Murchetach O'Brien was recognized by 1088 and lived until 1119, but from about 1103 his power was being challenged by Donal Mac Loughlin, and the northern king was still campaigning as late as 1115. Turlough O'Connor, king of Connacht (1119–56), had to overcome widespread opposition and was not secure as high king until the early 1130s. Even then he was challenged frequently by the Mac Loughlins, and by 1149 Murchetach Mac Loughlin was the most powerful figure in Irish politics. The struggle for power between Murchetach and Turlough's successor, Rory O'Connor, opened Ireland to the threat of foreign invasion.

The cause of future conflict lay in part in a quarrel between two lesser figures. In 1152, Dermot Mac Murrough, king of Leinster, abducted Dervorgilla, wife of Tiernan O'Rourke, king of Bréifne. She returned to her husband in the following year, but the episode left a legacy of animosity. Whether it was actually the motive for future policy is open to question. Dermot was allied with Murchetach Mac Loughlin while Tiernan supported Rory O'Connor. In 1166 Rory overthrew Murchetach and became high king, and Dermot had then to pay the price, both of his principal's failure and of his earlier misdeed. He was driven in exile from Leinster and, determined to regain his kingdom, he cast around for allies or mercenaries who might build up his military strength. At Bristol he was befriended by the wealthy and powerful citizen Robert fitz Harding and, perhaps through Robert's intervention, he secured Henry II's guarded patronage. From the king he received letters recording that 'if any person from within our wide domains is willing to help in restoring him, as one who has done fealty and homage to us, let him know that he has our good will and permission to do this'. Dermot found a response among the barons of south Wales. In particular, he secured a promise from Richard fitz Gilbert, who had much to gain from a successful intervention in Ireland but who had to move cautiously. His position was ambiguous; he used the style of earl, but was identified, not by Pembroke (as his father had been) but rather as Earl Richard of Strigoil. He had to ensure, on the one hand, that an Irish venture would bring him permanent advantages, and he gained that assurance when Dermot promised his daughter Eva in marriage and undertook that Richard should succeed him as king in Leinster. On the other hand, he had to be careful not to alienate Henry II, and until he had, as he thought, gained the king's permission, he would not embark for Leinster.

The early stages of Anglo-Norman intervention in southern Ireland were somewhat tentative (Martin, 1987). They deserve attention for three disparate reasons. One concerns the sources that cover them in detail. In *The Conquest of Ireland*, written less than twenty years after the invasion, Gerald of Wales concentrated especially on the achievements of his kinsmen in Ireland. *The Song of Dermot and the Earl*, a Norman French poem in circulation in the 1220s, has been described as the product of 'a skilful but naive craftsman'. It is well informed about the movements and activities of Dermot himself, and it has been suggested that it was based on a chronicle of events written by one of Dermot's administrators, his interpreter Maurice O'Regan. The second reason is that the introduction of so many of the fitz Geralds and of their neighbours from south-west Wales into Leinster was to have far-reaching consequences for southern Ireland. The third is that Norman ambitions in Leinster were the immediate occasion for Henry II's intervention in Irish affairs.

In 1167, a small group led by the Flemish lord of Roche accompanied Dermot to Leinster, but it was May 1169 before Robert fitz Stephen landed with a force of some 300 men. Hervey de Montmorency, Earl Richard's representative with that advance party, had a very small following, and they were soon joined by Maurice of Prendergast with about 200 men. Linking up with Dermot they attacked Wexford, which surrendered after a spirited show of defence. Robert received the town for himself and his half-brother, and Hervey was given land to the west of the town. Maurice of Prendergast, excluded at that stage from any landed settlement, was content for the present to fight for Dermot against Ossory. Rory O'Connor and his allies recognized Dermot's control over the southern part of Leinster, but Dermot's Norman force was weakened when Maurice took his contingent to serve as mercenaries for the king of Ossory. So closely was Maurice associated with this kingdom that he could be identified in contemporary records as Maurice of Ossory. In the short term he withdrew with his force to

Wales, but he would return later with Strongbow and establish himself and his successors in Ireland. The balance of power was restored in Dermot's favour later in 1169 when Maurice fitz Gerald landed with about 140 men. If Gerald of Wales is to be trusted, they were used for a brief campaign raiding and plundering around Dublin to remind the Norsemen of that city that Dermot's power was still a significant factor.

In 1170 the main force of the Anglo-Norman troops arrived. In May, Raymond le Gros, a younger son of the fitz Geralds of Carew, landed with an advance guard of ten knights and seventy archers at Baginbun, where they began to fortify their landing place with a series of earthworks along the cliff top. There they were attacked by the Norsemen from Waterford with a large body of Irish fighters. Numerically the odds were overwhelming, but by a mixture of guile and bravado le Gros routed the attackers. A herd of cattle was stampeded towards the Irish, and in the ensuing confusion the Normans made sallies and caused heavy casualties. Seventy citizens of Waterford were taken prisoner and, in a deliberate and callous act designed to strike terror in the city, were summarily executed; the living and dead alike were thrown over the cliffs. In August Earl Richard landed with the main body of his troops; estimates of their number vary between 1,500 and 2,000 men.

The first prize to fall to their combined forces was Waterford, where Dermot joined them and the marriage of Earl Richard and Eva was celebrated. Then they concentrated on Dublin and its environs; Raymond le Gros and Miles of Cogan made the decisive breach in the defences and the city fell. Within a year, in April 1171, Dermot died, and Strongbow could be seen, no longer as a mercenary commander or an ally, but as a claimant for the whole of Leinster. In successive attacks, Asgall, king of Dublin, and Rory O'Connor sought to regain Dublin, but the Anglo-Norman forces routed both armies. The courage, flair and opportunism that Raymond le Gros and Miles of Cogan so often displayed snatched victory from the prospect of almost certain failure. These were critical months during which Earl Richard faced open hostility from the Mac Murroughs and their allies, anxious to see the dynasty restored to power.

The earl had also to deal with direct intervention by Henry II. The king's interest in Ireland had been engaged as early as 1155, when an invasion of the island was being canvassed. Then, John of Salisbury was instrumental in securing papal support from Adrian IV, but the Irish expedition was not taken up as a matter of serious policy. Much more significant was Henry's hostile reaction to the invastions of 1169–70. Earl Richard was ordered to return to England, further supplies to Ireland were forbidden, and no one was to travel there without the king's permission. Henry's desire to establish a legitimate claim to Ireland cannot be questioned (see pp. 10–11). The means by which that was secured has been the subject of sustained enquiry. Gerald of Wales, writing in the 1180s, recorded in his *Conquest of Ireland*, the text of Pope Adrian's approval in his bull *Laudabiliter*, and he also recorded Alexander III's confirmation of the earlier concession. The authenticity of the two documents has been fiercely contested, as scholars seek to establish whether Gerald produced authentic texts, but Henry II had no doubt that his claim to Ireland was fully vindicated. Earl Richard sought to placate and reassure the king, first by sending Raymond le Gros as an ambassador, and then by travelling to Gloucestershire to meet the king in person.

During 1171 food supplies, animals and equipment were collected throughout England in preparation for an Irish campaign. In October Henry sailed with a large army. A scutage was levied, and while he was actively engaged in Ireland his sheriffs collected some £1,900 for his campaign. Once he had landed at Waterford, the expedition became more of a triumphal progress, as Anglo-Norman, Irish and Norse leaders joined him on peaceable and friendly terms. Robert fitz Stephen was then a prisoner in chains, and he received short shrift from the king until friends interceded for him. Strongbow was content to hold Leinster of the king for the service of 100 knights, but the king retained for the present Wexford, Waterford and Dublin. Irish kings from Cork, Desmond, Thomond, Bréifne, Oriel and Ulidia, together with representatives of the Mac Murroughs in Leinster, submitted to Henry. To hold Earl Richard in check the king gave Hugh de Lacy the kingdom of Meath as a lordship. From the Anglo-Norman side, he would have no single magnate as the dominant figure in Ireland. The dangers of this policy were exposed when Hugh de Lacy married a daughter of the reigning king of Meath without Henry II's permission; then all the dangers implicit in Strongbow's position in Leinster threatened to reappear in Meath. The complementary facet of Henry's policy emerged with the treaty of Windsor in 1175, by which Rory O'Connor accepted Henry as his overlord and Henry recognized in broad terms those parts of Ireland that lay within Rory's jurisdiction.

Henry II's intervention in Ireland established that Anglo-Norman settlers would act in Ireland under royal supervision and that they would be subject to English laws. Irish kings would accept his suzerainty and, in theory at least, enjoy his protection. Although the recognition of Rory O'Connor's standing as high king came in 1175, in practice Henry could not restrain the Anglo-Norman predators, and in 1177 he found it expedient to grant Cork to Robert fitz Stephen and Miles of Cogan, and Thomond to Philip de Braose. The protection he had offered to the Irish rulers was of little value. In fact, Dermot Mac Carthy could not be dislodged from Desmond, and Philip de Braose could make no headway in Thomond.

The fortunes of war were very different in the north. When Strongbow died in 1176 the king sent William fitz Audelin to take control of Leinster during the minority of the earl's son. One of his associates was a Somerset knight, John de Courcy. Gerald of Wales wrote approvingly of his gentle and attractive character and of his skills as a commander who liked to be in the thick of an engagement. After only a few months in Dublin, John gathered a force of twenty-two knights and some 300 troops, said to be discontented with conditions there, and set out for the northern kingdom of Ulaidh (Ulidia). He met with strong resistance from the ruler, Rory Mac Dunlevy, before he took Rory's principal base at Downpatrick in January 1177, and he had to deal with renewed and persistent opposition as he extended his conquests northwards. Secure in Ulidia, he turned south-west in an attempt to absorb the small kingdom of Argialla (Oriel), but his success there was limited, and in the thirteenth century the area was distinguished as English

Oriel and Irish Oriel. The fierce resistance to de Courcy's advance is reflected in the number of castles that were built to defend his conquests. They extended from Carlingford, Newry and Dundrum in the south to Carrickfergus and Coleraine in the north. At Carrickfergus what was to become the inner ward of the thirteenth-century castle represents his work. At Dundrum he constructed a deep ditch to supplement the natural defences of the site, and there his work is now the upper ward of the castle. The earliest buildings at Carlingford are associated, not with John de Courcy, but with Hugh de Lacy.

John de Courcy was never given formal licence to create this lordship, though Henry II may have made some informal and ambiguous remark implying approval. Relations between the Anglo–Norman settlers and the local Irish dynasties in and near Ulidia were not consistently hostile. John proved to be a useful ally, especially for Aedh O'Neill, the most formidable of the northern Irish leaders. Unlike other successful commanders, John did not marry into any of the local dynasties; instead he married Affreca, daughter of the Manx king Gottred, and established long-lasting links with the Norse dynasty and southern Scotland. Part of his strength lay in the prospect of a fleet he could call upon from his father-in-law, and as part of his tactics for exploiting the resources of his lordship he imported a working force from southern Scotland and added to the racial mix in Ireland.

For twenty-seven years John remained secure in Ulidia, and the extent to which he had identified himself with his Irish lordship can be seen from the religious foundations he established. At Downpatrick three communities were founded: Benedictines from Chester, Augustinians from Carlisle and a group of brothers of the Holy Cross (themselves following the Rule of St Augustine); at Carrickfergus Premonstratensians from Dryburgh; at St Andrews in Ards Benedictines; at Inch Cistercians from Furness. Small wonder that he could exercise a powerful influence in northern Ireland. He was a loyal and useful administrator, serving Henry II as justiciar in Ireland in 1185 and remaining loyal to Richard I despite Prince John's intrigues. That was not likely to be forgotten once John became king, and as the thirteenth century opened his position weakened. He had been striking coins in his own name, and the not inaccurate but dangerous title of prince of Ulidia was being used to describe his power. In Hugh de Lacy the younger he had an ambitious and dangerous neighbour who could count on King John for support. From 1201 until 1204 Hugh undermined his position and in May 1205 defeated him in a decisive encounter. King John made Hugh earl of Ulster and gave him the lands held by de Courcy 'on the day when Hugh defeated him' at Dundrum. John de Courcy, set free after a brief imprisonment, lived until 1219, but he was a man without influence.

The establishment of large fiefs in Ireland under royal lordship had important financial implications for the English crown. The great fiefs were burdened with knight service, often on a heavy scale: so, for example, Leinster owed 100 knights, Cork and Limerick each owed sixty, Meath was initially assessed at fifty knights, Philip of Prendergast's lordship in Munster owed forty, and Theobald Walter's fief, centred on his castle of Nenagh, was assessed at twenty-two fees. Whether by raising men or raising money through scutage, Ireland could contribute materially to the crown's resources, and in the thirteenth century Irish manpower and money could be used to implement royal policy in Wales and in Gascony. The great magnates in Ireland made sure of ample military strength by enfeoffing many more than their quota of knights on their estates.

When such men as Earl Richard and Hugh de Lacy enfeoffed knights in their lordships, their motive in the short term was to secure their conquests, but their dispositions had long-term consequences, for the men to whom they gave fiefs established families which survived for generations. The pattern can be seen very clearly in terms of the fitz Geralds and their connections endowed by Earl Richard in Leinster. Maurice fitz Gerald was given Naas and a cantred in Ui Fáeláin. His four sons grew to manhood and inherited or acquired rich estates, while his daughter married Hervey de Montmorency. His eldest son William succeeded Maurice at Naas in 1176, and when he himself died without children, early in the thirteenth century, his brother Gerald inherited that fief. Gerald married Eva de Bermingham, who brought him the lordship of Offaly. From Hamo of Valognes he gained Croom. Hamo also enfeoffed a third son of Maurice fitz Gerald at Shanid; a fourth son had nominal claims to lands in Tyrconnell and was to have a profitable career as an administrator. Their sister Nest married Hervey de Montmorency, but they did not establish a family; Hervey became a monk and died without heirs. In later generations, marriage, inheritance, new grants and judicious purchases of land extended the dynasty's wealth in Waterford, Desmond, Kerry, Limerick and Sligo.

Other fitz Gerald connections received estates in the lordship. Meiler fitz Henry, whose career in Ireland spanned the years 1170–1208 and who served as justiciar in the last years of his life, was given lands which later became the barony of Carbury. He left no children and his estates passed to his cousin, Gerald fitz Maurice. Miles, son of the bishop of St David's, David fitz Gerald, was given lands which his heirs held as the barony of Iverk, in Ossory. Two more fitz Geralds were well endowed, Raymond le Gros and his brother Gruffydd (whose name occurs consistently in Irish historical writing as Griffin). Raymond received the two baronies of Forth and Idrone, which represented the territory of the O'Nolans in Fothairt and the O'Ryans in Ui Dróna. His lands in Leinster were given to his nephew William fitz Odo of Carew, and passed to the Carews of Idrone. He left another successor, Richard, presumably an illegitimate son, through whom his conquests in Cork passed to the Carews of Cork. Griffin had a less spectacular endowment: he acquired Knocktopher, where the motte of his castle survived until 1973.

There is some danger in concentrating on one extended family in this context. Strongbow and his successors, the Marshals, were served by men from many parts of France and England. Gilbert de Boisrohard, from Bosc-le-Hard in north-eastern Normandy, was given the barony of Ballaghkeen, and Robert de Quincy, whose family roots were in Picardy, became Earl Richard's constable, with the lordship of Duffry. The Quincy family gained land, wealth and influence in England and Scotland, as well as in Ireland. One of the earl's most constant companions, John de Clahull, held the important castle of Leighlen with twenty fees; he was probably from a family settled in Bedfordshire. Another castellan, at Castledermot, was Walter de Ridelsford, who hailed from Yorkshire.

The Lacy subjugation of Meath may be used to illustrate a different aspect of Anglo-Norman settlement, the effects of conquest on leading Irish families. Hugh de Lacy underlined the eclipse of the O'Melaghlin dynasty as kings of Meath by keeping Dun-na-Sciath, their royal seat, in his own hands. The title of king was not used after the assassination of Art O'Melaghlin in 1185, and the family's tenure was limited to the barony of Clonlanon on the western edge of the lordship. Lesser dynasties whose territories lay on the fringes of the lordship survived for centuries: the O'Reillys of Cavan, the O'Farrells of Annaly, the O'Molloys in land south of Athlone, the O'Carrolls of Ely (south of Birr), and the Mageoghegans of Keneliagh. Those whose lands had been in the central area of Meath had little hope of surviving; they may be identified as sometime kings of Gailenga, Luigni and Delbna. The name of the last dynasty survives in the place-name Delvin, but it is significant that Delvin is the site of one of the strongest Anglo-Norman castles of the lordship. There is nothing here, or in the rest of Ireland, to compare with Earl Richard's treatment in Leinster of his Irish brother-in-law Donal, who continued to hold the royal residence at Liamhain and was regarded as an Anglo-Norman baron. His descendants took the style, which became the family name, FitzDermot.

Royal lordship was given firm expression when the young Prince John was appointed as lord of Ireland. His early visit in 1185 was planned on a lavish scale; English sheriffs raised well over £400 towards his expenses. It was significant especially because, with his train of 300 knights, John brought with him new men whose families would play an important role in Irish affairs in the future. William de Burgh (*de Burgo*) acquired a small landed base around Athassel, and, with conquests made further afield, his successors would long be powerful in Connacht and Ulster. Theobald Walter, John's butler, who was granted land in Thomond, was the ancestor of the Butler family, their possessions being mainly in Tipperary and the south-west. Philip of Worcester was also established in Tipperary with Cahir as his chief stronghold, where his family survived in the male line until 1275. In the north John's seneschal, Bertram of Verdon, was given a small but strategically important fief centred on Dundalk, with another newcomer, Gilbert Pipard, as his neighbour at Ardee. There they could share in the exploitation of Oriel and form an effective check, first on John de Courcy's ambitions and then on Hugh de Lacy's control of Ulster.

The pattern of Anglo-Norman domination of Ireland was reinforced: adventurers, arriving as mercenaries who might acquire lands and fortune in Ireland, were supplemented by magnates introduced into Ireland and given lands there through the patronage of Henry II, acting on his own behalf or, later, on behalf of Prince John. A number of these families identified themselves very closely with their Irish lands. The clearest example is that of the Lacy family. Hugh de Lacy came to Ireland with Henry II in 1171; he was given Meath, and entrusted with wide authority – a justiciar in practice if not in name. When rebellion against Henry II broke out in England and his French lordships in 1173, Lacy was recalled to help put down the revolt, but once order had been restored he returned to Ireland. By 1177 his English estates had become a secondary interest. He was assassinated at Durrow in 1186, and his three sons, all under age, had to wait some years before the king would hand over control of their inheritances, but they remained deeply involved in the politics of Anglo-Norman Ireland until the 1240s.

King John's main ally in Ireland was William Marshal (Painter, 1933); he married Strongbow's heiress in 1189 but had to wait until after 1204 before he could play a full part in Irish affairs. In politics he was generally cautious, though not afraid to be outspoken, and despite many provocations was consistently loyal to the Angevin kings. Two magnates aroused John's suspicions, William de Braose, lord of Limerick, and the younger Hugh de Lacy, earl of Ulster. They represented a single problem, for William de Braose and his family fled to Ireland, and while William went to France they found refuge with Hugh de Lacy. In 1210 John mounted a vigorous campaign in Ireland. He landed near Waterford, marched through Leinster and reached Dublin as his main base. Walter de Lacy was deprived of Meath and had to wait until 1215 before he was reinstated. Hugh de Lacy, primarily a threat because of his power in Ulster, was attacked for harbouring Matilda de Braose and found himself completely outclassed by the king. John opened his campaign by capturing the castle of Carlingford and then taking Dundrum, while part of his army crossed by sea to the mountains of Mourne and took Hugh's northern stronghold at Carrickfergus. Antrim surrendered, and John could leave Ireland with his authority enhanced by a successful campaign. In Ireland he displayed all the qualities that marked his campaign against Mirabeau in 1202, and which were so signally lacking in the crucial campaigns in France in 1204 and 1214.

More important than the settlement of tenurial issues was the reinforcement of the place of Dublin in Irish politics. Since 1170 the city had been the centre of royal authority, and the castle established there by Miles of Cogan had been an important royal stronghold. John commissioned new work on the castle, parts of which can still be seen in the foundations of the present complex of buildings. From 1170 onwards Dublin, protected by a ring of defensive castles, emerged steadily as a bastion of royal power. There lay the centre of royal government and influence. One clear indication of Anglo-Norman domination was the succession of archbishops of Dublin more acceptable to the English administration than to the Irish population. By a slow process, English law and procedures were introduced through Dublin. In 1204 the justiciar in Ireland was empowered to issue a series of judicial writs on his own authority, and in 1246 Henry III decreed that all the writs of common law available in England should also be available in Ireland. A comprehensive collection of writs was sent to Dublin so that there could be no doubt of the procedures to be followed. With the introduction of English law there went the gradual introduction of shires and shire courts. Pressure on Irish rulers was sustained. The area of independent Irish rule in the north was steadily reduced and Anglo-Norman forces advanced to the west, first to the line of the Shannon and then beyond that natural barrier. The kingdom of Connacht retained a formal but insecure independence until, in 1235, leading settlers from Anglo-Norman Ireland invaded it and seized fresh lands there.

One consequence of the small number of settler families in Ireland was a gradual absorption of 'English' families into an Irish way of life (Frame, 1981). With the descendants of one of Hugh de Lacy's honorial baronage, Jocelin de Angulo, this transition had begun before the end of the twelfth century. Jocelin's estates centred on Navan; he took part in the conquest of Meath, and his son Gilbert was active in the Lacy advance into Ulster. But Gilbert also took service with the king of Connacht, Cathal Crovderg O'Connor, who gave him land in Roscommon. His patronymic, fitz Jocelin, was translated into Irish as Mac Goisdelbh, and the process of adopting Irish ways and Irish outlook was continued by his successors. They could be matched by other settler families: the Berminghams in their barony of Dunmore, the Costantins of Kilbixy, the Poers who became Mac Pheorais, and the family of St Aubyn who became the Tobins. By the 1290s such families could be described as degenerate English, and in 1297 a belated attempt was made to curb by legislation the use of Irish dress and the fashion for long hair. The steady process by which an Anglo–Norman elite became an Anglo-Irish aristocracy was already discernible before the end of John's reign.

When they arrived in Ireland the Anglo–Norman invaders found two very different types of urban community. One was the large monastic site which housed a civilian population (see p. 98). The other was the coastal town established by Scandinavian settlers, the Ostmen, who formed a distinctive element in Irish society. Of these, Dublin was the largest centre. From Dublin itself, the Norse settlers had taken over a substantial hinterland, *Dyfflinarskiri* as they called it, and they had established ports along the coast, notably at Wicklow and Arklow. Further south they founded Wexford and the more substantial town at Waterford, where parts of the Scandinavian defences still survive. At Cork, as at Dublin, they first despoiled a monastery and later settled in the area. On the west coast, at Limerick, another important settlement flourished. In each case, the settlement extended beyond the town into the neighbouring countryside, described in later charters as their cantred and identified at Waterford as the foreigners' land (*Galltir*). There were smaller ports, which did not develop to the same degree, at

Annagassen in Dundalk Bay to the north, for example, and Dungarvan, with its sheltered harbour, between Waterford and Cork.

Dublin profited from the fact that Henry II retained the town in his own hands and made it the centre of royal authority. It had close links with Bristol, and Bristol merchants may already have established a small community there before the Anglo-Norman invasions. In 1172 the king gave Dublin formally to his men of Bristol, and the Irish town received the customs of Bristol. Prince John recognized the merchant gild, gave the townsmen their own court and confirmed their monopoly over local trade. By 1215 they had gained the right to elect their own reeve. By the early thirteenth century the population of Dublin was cosmopolitan, with Irish merchants, Ostmen families and a number of men from London and Bristol: there were many from south Wales and the border shires, others had come from the midlands and south-west England, and a few were drawn from Flanders and France. In the earliest years of the conquest a castle had been established there, with Miles of Cogan as castellan. Henry II added a ceremonial hall in 1171–2, and in John's reign this complex was greatly extended with a large stone-built castle. That Bristol should have been the pattern for the growth of the borough at Dublin need cause no surprise. Henry II had spent part of his boyhood – perhaps an impressionable part, limited though it was to about eighteen months – at Bristol castle, which was also the centre of John's principal honor, the earldom of Gloucester. Waterford, Cork and Limerick enjoyed royal patronage and before the end of the century they, too, had been granted the customs of Bristol.

Immigrant magnates were well aware of the advantages of creating and fostering urban communities. Richard fitz Gilbert in the 1170s and William Marshal in the first decade of the thirteenth century were familiar with small but prosperous boroughs at Chepstow and Pembroke. Under their protection a town developed outside the defences of their castle at Kilkenny, and further south Marshal built New Ross. Both towns were granted the customs of Breteuil. Hugh de Lacy had historic links with a major borough at Ludlow and was actively concerned with smaller communities at

Leominster and Weobley. In Ireland he founded a borough outside
Millmont, his castle at Drogheda, and a second community was
established on the opposite bank of the Boyne. The townsmen
living around Millmont were granted the customs of Breteuil by
Walter de Lacy in 1194; John confirmed the grant to both boroughs
in 1213, and later Henry III gave them full burghal status with the
right to elect their own officials. (Technically they remained as
separate boroughs, rather as in England two separate boroughs
grew up at Bristol and Redcliffe on the river Avon.)

John de Courcy encouraged the growth of a town at
Carrickfergus and another, probably smaller, community at
Downpatrick; nearby, the Verdons established a town at Dundalk,
which had to wait until the fourteenth century for the grant of
privileges – the clearest mark of borough status and of a community
large enough to be viable. Some twenty towns scattered through
Meath, Leinster and eastern Munster received the customs of
Breteuil in the thirteenth century. The full list would include major
centres at Clonmel, Dungarvan, Naas, Kildare and Trim. Beyond
that range of boroughs, smaller towns at such places as Cashel,
Nenagh, Thurles and Mullingar were given more restricted privileges and should probably be regarded as minor communities with
some potential for growth. The contrast in urban development
within the approximate limits 1160–1250 is quite remarkable.

Even at an early stage of this development, Gerald of Wales
identified Anglo-Norman towns as a cause of deep resentment
among the Irish. Boroughs were plainly centres of alien influence.
Their merchants and craftsmen were concerned with profit for
themselves and not with the community as a whole; he considered
the wealth engendered by trade should have been used for the
benefit of the whole of the Anglo-Norman lordship in Ireland. The
settlers were generous benefactors for the Irish church. Before
1230 they had established eighty new foundations; fourteen
Cistercian houses and twenty-six Augustinian monasteries gave
new impetus to the Irish monastic movement encouraged by
Malachy and his successors. But the greater number of these
houses were established in urban centres and were clearly linked
with Anglo-Norman power.

In the countryside, as Gerald noted, Irish leaders who had accepted the Normans as allies found them treacherous and greedy,
and mutual distrust was the inevitable result. It is not difficult to
see the steady build up of hostility; it is much more difficult to
assess the scale of this hostility in the twelfth and early thirteenth
centuries. There is a danger we may see the racial tensions of this
period in terms more appropriate to a later century. The increasing
pressure of lordship in the later middle ages, the invasion of the
north, sponsored by Robert Bruce and carried out by Edward
Bruce in 1315, the resurgence of English interest in Ireland in the
reign of Richard II and the exclusion of native-born Irish from a
number of principal towns in the fifteenth century – all made for
increasing friction. Still later the potent mixture of dynastic and
religious policies under the Tudors and Stuarts exacerbated older
tensions and multiplied the racial problems of Anglo-Irish society.
All that can introduce emotional overtones and distortions into our
interpretation of Anglo-Norman Ireland.

6

Architecture: Military and Ecclesiastical

The wide span of time which separates the Norman invasion of England in 1066 and the consolidation of Anglo-Norman control in Ireland, or of royal power in Scotland, in the early decades of the thirteenth century, witnessed a series of building styles in secular and ecclesiastical architecture. In earlier chapters we have been concerned with the use of castles and churches and with their place in political and cultural development; here we are concerned with the buildings themselves.

With castles and domestic buildings, site and function often determined the style, and the resources the king or a great magnate was prepared to put into a particular castle determined the scale (Pounds, 1990). Different types of defence overlapped and re-curred. The motte, with strong wood-built defences, characteristic of periods of conquest and settlement, remained a permanent feature in Scotland for much of the thirteenth century. Stone-built defences appeared very early in England, with some of the most important Norman castles dating from the first years of the con-quest. There was a steady proliferation of stone castles right through to the end of the twelfth century (Brown, 1989). In Scotland the royal dynasty could afford large stone castles, cer-tainly at Edinburgh and Stirling, and a major palace at Dunferm-line, but Scottish magnates were less able, or less willing, to invest heavily, and very few stone castles can be assigned to the twelfth century. Even in the thirteenth century, when such castles acquired a substantial prestige value, very few were built in Scotland until the threat of Edward I's ambitions had to be countered. In Wales and Ireland the constant demands of defence made strong castles essential. It is rare to find a castle completely demolished and rebuilt in a new style. Changes were made by adaptation and extension, and sometimes castellans were reluctant even to demolish more than was absolutely essential to make room for improvements. The historian's basic task is, then, to unravel the sequence of buildings on any particular site. From the 1260s onwards a major change can be discerned; then, new castles, designed by expert architects and built by a large work-force, introduce a new phase of military architecture. But that lies well beyond the limits of Anglo-Norman expansion.

Where churches are concerned, there is less sense of unity over the whole period. The style that, in England, is often called Norman, but which is better described here, as on the continent, as Romanesque, is characteristic of the late eleventh century. It can be identified by the use of rounded arches, massive supports and heavy, if not solid, walling. By the third quarter of the twelfth century it would begin to give way to the more graceful style classified as Early English, in which the pointed arch and lancet windows would open up new possibilities for designers and masons to exploit. Early Norman foundations in Wales saw the Romanesque style firmly established there. In Ireland the churches built by Anglo-Norman settlers continued to be Romanesque surprisingly late in the twelfth century, with a change of style emerging early in the thirteenth. Then, chancels marked by a stately row of tall lancet windows became a characteristic feature of Irish monasteries and cathedral churches.

When patrons could find new money for enlarging and enhancing churches, the tendency was generally to start by rebuilding the eastern end of a church, the sanctuary, chancel and choir, and then if possible to work through the transepts and nave to the west front. Sometimes the process was carried through completely, but often it was checked and only part of the church rebuilt. So it is common to find a thirteenth-century chancel and choir marking the new phase, with a Romanesque nave little altered.

Military Architecture

The great stone keeps of the Norman kings derive from the castles they knew in Normandy, from Fécamp, Caen and Falaise, and especially from Rouen (where the keep was demolished in 1204). London and Colchester were founded very early in the Conqueror's reign; at London three sites were fortified late in 1066 in readiness for William I to be safe in the city, and Colchester was founded in 1067. Work on Colchester's keep probably began between 1074 and 1076; the building of the Tower of London is said to have been started in 1078, and it was completed in 1097. The Tower was designed by Gundulf, a monk of Bec, who later became bishop of Rochester. Norwich was founded in 1067, and it seems likely that the keep was built by Henry I and modelled on the castle he knew well at Falaise. Norwich had its principal accommodation on two storeys, Colchester and the Tower on three. Their appearance has been changed over the centuries. Colchester lost its upper storey and battlements in the seventeenth century, while the Tower was given an additional storey and needed major restoration again in the nineteenth century. Norwich was embellished by an elaborate pattern of blank arcading on its outer walls, but these, badly weathered, were replaced when the keep was refaced between 1833 and 1839.

These large keeps had two advantages: they provided room for spacious living quarters, as well as for a garrison and a large staff, and they were very difficult to capture. The thickness of the walls and the scale of the building made them virtually impregnable. The entrance was at first floor level, and it could only be reached by a staircase protected by a strong forebuilding.

It was a type of castle building that remained popular. As part of the attempt to defend northern England, Ranulph Flambard, bishop of Durham, built a castle at Norham in 1121. Within twenty years it had been destroyed by the Scots, and in 1157 Bishop Hugh de Puiset set about building a stronger castle with extensive defences and strong gatehouses (Meirion-Jones and Jones, 1993). The core of his castle was a large tower keep with three storeys, still impressive as a ruin, and in its prime formidable.

He was by no means the only prominent cleric to be involved in this way. William of Corbeil, archbishop of Canterbury, was responsible for building the great keep at Rochester, where Gundulf had built the earlier defences. William d'Aubigny built a splendid example at Castle Rising in 1138, and the de Vere family established a tower keep at Castle Hedingham in 1141. Henry II, familiar with the great *donjons* of Anjou, built tower keeps at two of his best-known castles at Newcastle upon Tyne and Dover. They are of particular interest because one of the king's military architects, Maurice, is known to have worked on both castles; they share the common feature that the forebuilding rises, not to first floor level, but to the second floor, and that is presumably a detail of design peculiar to this architect. Henry II was spending money on the fortifications at Dover from 1168 until the end of his reign in 1189, and the keep itself was built between 1181 and 1188 at an estimated cost of £4,000. Newcastle was built a decade earlier, between 1172 and 1177, at the much lower cost of some £900.

The use of stone in a range of castles occurs early in the Conqueror's reign. To hold down the city of Exeter, Baldwin de Meules was established there in 1068 as sheriff. He acquired Okehampton, where he built a motte with a square stone tower, both of which have been dated to *c*.1068. At Chepstow work on the hall-keep and its curtain wall was started before 1071. At the major castle at Corfe, established by the Conqueror, the defensive wall may have been of stone, and a rectangular tower keep had been added by about 1100. The important castle that the Lacy family established at Ludlow is recorded in 1091, and parts of the curtain walling and flanking towers are eleventh century in date. So, too, is the curtain wall of Peveril castle, built in the wild country of the Peak district before 1086; a small keep was added in 1176.

One of the most attractive smaller castles to survive is to be found at Restormel. There, about 1100, a very strong earthern ringwork with a stone gatehouse was built. Later in the twelfth century a shell keep was built on the earthwork, converting it into a more orthodox structure, but the earlier stonework survived. Shell keeps reproduced in stone one type of wooden tower which gave the motte its strength. A low circular wall provided defence and protected an area within which domestic accommodation could be built, often as lean-to buildings around the inner face of the wall. Tamworth castle had been established before 1086 as a motte and bailey castle, and in the early twelfth century a shell keep was added to the motte. It survives, with evidence of successive conversions, the inner space now crowded with later buildings, while the bailey has long since disappeared. At Arundel, where the motte has existed since 1094, William d'Aubigny added a shell keep with a finely decorated entry in or about 1138. That could be matched by the shell keep Ivo de Vesci built at Alnwick in the middle decades of the twelfth century. As Arundel was extended to be the principal residence of a great magnate, the motte and keep became a decorative feature, with the great house developing in the two baileys of the castle, while at Alnwick (as at Berkeley), the keep itself became the nucleus of the great house of the later middle ages.

Small rectangular keeps, strong but modest in scale, were the principal strong point in a number of castles. Three examples from different areas of England may illustrate their use. At Porchester, within the old Roman fortifications, a small rectangular fortified house was built, late in the eleventh century. It then consisted of a single-storey building, though its modest scale may have disguised a significant function. Under Henry I it was held by Robert Mauduit, a chamberlain of the exchequer, and, as occasional entries in the Pipe Rolls make clear, Henry II used it as a depot for shipping treasure to Normandy. King John found it useful for the prosaic but essential function of storing wine! The defences were strengthened in Richard I's reign; the walls were made thicker, the height was increased at least twice during the twelfth century, converting it into a substantial keep, and the entrance and the surrounding bailey were extended to make a strong and comfortable residence. At Goodrich a small but beautifully proportioned keep, probably dating from the early twelfth century, was the nucleus of this border castle on the Wye. Early in the thirteenth century the Marshal family acquired it and refashioned it as a formidable concentric castle, with heavy drum towers and a well-guarded approach and entry. They did not demolish the earlier keep, which remained as an old-fashioned but still useful part of the accommodation available for their use. Though it was necessary in conditions of war, it was no easy job to remove such a keep; to demolish it as part of a rebuilding programme might be a costly luxury. It was done at Whitecastle, in the lordship of the three castles in Gwent. A square Norman keep survived and was still being repaired for use as late as 1257, but in the 1260s, with the prospect of major hostilities in Wales, Whitecastle was no longer regarded as an adequate defence for the border. It was completely rebuilt as a major concentric castle, and the old keep was demolished; its foundations remain, with the curtain wall of the new castle built across them.

The greatest weakness of the rectangular keep was the risk that the corners might be mined: a tunnel would be dug beneath the corner, filled with brushwood and set on fire. If it succeeded, the foundations would give way, and the corner, with a large part of the walling on both sides, would collapse. That happened when King John laid siege to Rochester in 1215. The south-east corner of the keep was mined and collapsed, and when the castle was repaired the square corner was replaced by a round tower: if the tower had no sharp angle, the danger of mining was much reduced.

The value of round towers was recognized at a comparatively early date; perhaps they should be regarded as an extension of the use of shell keeps. William d'Aubigny was responsible for the erection of a new castle at Buckenham in or about 1138, a castle marked by a circular keep, which is believed to be the earliest round keep built in England. They are quite common, though it is not always easy to date them precisely. In Wales, the Clifford family's round keep at Bronllys was built in the mid-1160s. Mahel of Hereford, lord of Brecknock, was killed there in 1165 by a stone that fell from the keep, then being constructed.

At Orford in Suffolk – a shire dominated by the Bigod earls of Norfolk – Henry II constructed a highly individual castle, which was said to be one of his favourites. It was built at a cost of £1,400 between 1165 and 1173, with a keep and extensive outer works. The inside of the keep was circular, but the exterior wall was made up of a number of flat surfaces forming a polygonal tower. The structure was supported by three massive buttresses, which not only gave it strength but contributed to its distinctive appearance. Something similar was achieved at Conisborough in Yorkshire, where Henry II's half-brother, Hamelin de Warenne, built a keep based on his castle at Mortemer in Normandy. It was a circular tower, rising four storeys, but it was dominated by six buttresses, which both sustained it and disguised its basic shape. The round tower that elicits most admiration from historians was built by William Marshal at Pembroke about 1200. The castle occupies the end of a spur, heavily defended on the town side and enclosed by an impressive sequence of walls and towers. They represent an earlier line of defence but may have been extensively rebuilt by the Earl Marshal. His tower survives, still with its unusual stone domed roof, dwarfing the complex of domestic buildings around it.

At Pembroke the large space enclosed by the curtain walling left ample room for new buildings, but at another Welsh castle modernization had to be achieved on a constricted site. The core of the Picard's castle at Tretower was a motte, reinforced by stone revetment, on which a shell keep was built. In the early thirteenth century the interior of the keep was gutted and a large round tower was built inside the shell; domestic buildings were fitted into the narrow space between the old and the new work. The site was low-lying and marshy, and the motte occupied the highest ground; there was no obvious alternative site for the new tower.

The ruins of domestic buildings built in the thirteenth century survive in the baileys of many castles: a hall, a kitchen range, a chapel and other ancillary buildings. At Pembroke two halls were built, one by William Marshal, the other a generation later. With the spacious accommodation in these halls, the keep and the gatehouse, the castle was a large and luxurious residence. The exceptional scale of royal building may be seen in Westminster hall, where the east and west walls survive from William Rufus's work (1097–9), or in the great hall at Winchester, first built in the twelfth century but given its present form in the reign of Henry III. The hall of Oakham castle, dating from *c*.1160, has survived intact and has been carefully preserved, and the substantial remains of another hall, built about the same time, have survived at Christchurch.

Stone castles built by Norman lords in Wales are much over-shadowed by the great concentric castles of the Edwardian conquest. A number were deliberately replaced, as Bagillt was superseded by Flint. In the middle March, the most important castles were in English shires: Richard's Castle and Longtown, both impressive ruins, held key positions; much of Clun's well-developed fortifications survive, while only fragments remain of Bishop's Castle and Hopton. Ruins surviving in south Wales are more extensive. In the twelfth century rectangular keeps were built at Monmouth and Usk, for example, and at exposed castle sites at Ogmore and Coity, Norman halls at Barry and Manorbier, and walls and towers at Caldicot and Newcastle (Bridgend). In the thirteenth century rectangular keeps were added to fortifications at Abergavenny and Loughor, and circular keeps were built at Brecon, Caldicot and Llandovery. The defensive network of the lordship of Brecknock is still clear to see. With their outlying castles strongly fortified, the lords of Glamorgan were comparatively slow to build their shell keep at Cardiff. William Marshal's rich inheritance in south Wales gave him the opportunity to overhaul a number of castles. He modernized the defences of Usk and Cardigan and made modest additions to Chepstow; Pembroke he transformed. His successor was responsible for the impressive inner bailey of Cilgerran castle in the 1220s.

From the second half of the twelfth century, two developments may be traced. One was to add to castles already well defended an outer defence of strong curtain walling with flanking towers. Between 1180 and 1189 Henry II provided such a defensive ring for his keep at Dover, with rectangular flanking towers, and he began to build an ambitious outer bailey, which still retains some rectangular towers. In the thirteenth century the characteristic mural tower would be circular. The other development was to create a strong-hold which depended, not upon a keep, but upon the strength of its curtain wall and flanking towers. At Framlingham, the site of the

Bigods' castle is dominated by a strong curtain wall with thirteen rectangular towers. It has no keep, no final refuge; the entire enclosure forms the strong point of the castle. This was an adaptation of the circular inner ward of a castle, long disputed between the king and the Bigod earl of Norfolk, which was captured and demolished by Henry II in 1174. The Bigods did not regain possession of the castle until 1189, and the new work was then put in hand. It retained an extensive range of outer defences of earthworks and wooden palisades throughout the thirteenth century, but the main strength of the castle lay in the impressive stone enceinte built in the 1190s.

This development, with large circular or D-shaped towers dominating massive curtain walls, became commonplace during the thirteenth century. It may be seen in comparatively simple form at Pevensey, where about 1220 a new gatehouse with projecting drum towers was the first stage in new defences, which were completed in the middle years of the century. Chepstow's defences were strengthened at the end of the twelfth century with large drum towers to guard the eastern outer wall, and between about 1225 and 1245 this area of the castle was extended with the present lower bailey, a massive gatehouse, and a large circular tower – almost a *donjon* in itself. We are not far removed from the pioneering concentric castles of Kidwelly and Caerphilly.

In Scotland early stone castles are rare. In part, that may be due to the fact that a number of castles were demolished, particularly in later phases of Anglo-Scottish warfare, and rebuilt in new styles. The small Romanesque chapel at Edinburgh castle, thought to have been built early in the twelfth century and later associated with St Margaret, suggests stone defences from at least the beginning of the twelfth century; literary evidence indicates an earlier date, before the queen's death in 1093. At Stirling, the royal chapel is mentioned in 1150, and that too suggests a stone-built castle established in the first half of the twelfth century. Before 1200 they could be matched by fragments of the north-west tower of Aberdour castle and the major stone defences at Invernochty and Lumphanan. It is salutary to recall that the two earliest surviving stone keeps in Scotland were not built under Norman patronage.

About 1145, at Wyre in the Orkneys, the Norse leader Kolbein Hruga built a stone castle, Cobbie Row's castle, of which the lower courses survive. In Argyll, at Castle Sween, stand the ruins of another rectangular keep, probably built early in the thirteenth century.

The castle built at Rothesay by William, son of Alan, or his successors presents critical problems of dating. The earliest work consists of a massive earthen ringwork, on which a circular stone defence was built. In its thirteenth-century format it was reinforced by four circular towers, and somewhat later a gatehouse and extensive outworks made the castle very formidable. Douglas Simpson consistently regarded Rothesay as a thirteenth-century fortification in depth (Simpson, 1959). A. A. M. Duncan (1975) is inclined to place the early stonework in the second half of the twelfth century, some time after 1164, and to identify it as a shell keep, much altered in later decades; it would be the only one of its kind to be found in Scotland.

The first half of the thirteenth century produced a small number of fine concentric castles. The stronghold of the earls of Mar at Kildrummy, where building began between 1223 and 1245, has a *donjon*, three mural towers and strong curtain walls. It was extended in the late thirteenth century, and the gatehouse is attributed to Edward I's distinguished castle-builder, James of St George. Dirleton, on a site already being fortified by the de Vaux family before 1225, retains a substantial amount of thirteenth-century work; so too does Inverlochy. They may stand for the limited investment in large stone castles in Scotland in the early thirteenth century.

The invasion of Ireland produced a renewed spate of castle-building, with many ringworks and mottes, and over a period of about seventy-five years, in round terms from 1170 until 1245, many of these were transformed into stone-built fortresses. Some fine examples survive to demonstrate the scale and variety of castle-building during this seminal period (Rae, 1987).

One castle in particular, Carrickfergus, was built in three phases. It may have been the earliest stone castle built by the Anglo-Norman settlers, and stone defences, presumably on the line of what is now the inner bailey, may have existed as early as 1178. Within the next four years John de Courcy began to build the large keep and the inner bailey. The rectangular keep, a classic three-storey building with corner turrets and a floor area of some 325 square yards, was built into the north-west corner of the polygonal bailey, which was strongly constructed, without mural towers. Where de Courcy found his builder or the inspiration for his keep cannot be guessed; there was no obvious source in his native Somerset. This castle served as the basic northern defence of Ulster until it was besieged by King John in 1210. Then John de Courcy added the present middle ward to strengthen the coastal defence to the south-west and to provide a narrow bailey for the keep itself. The third and final phase, built between 1228 and 1242 by Hugh de Lacy, provided defences for the whole of the promontory on which the castle was built and, especially, the strongly defended gatehouse which controlled the landward approach.

A number of rectangular keeps, designed on a smaller scale, were built in the thirteenth century. The ruins of the keep built on the western edge of the monastic enclave at Clonmacnois may belong to the first decade of the century; so too may the keeps at Cahir and Maynooth, both much altered in later centuries. The purpose of the keep built at Greencastle was to guard the ferry-link with Carlingford, and it must surely be linked with the younger Hugh de Lacy, and so be dated well before 1243. The style of the surviving stonework of the Pipard's keep at Ardee suggests an early date. The castle at Athenry was built in the course of the invasion of Galway by Gerald de Bermingham in 1238, and the keep at Seafin has been dated as late as 1252. This leaves out of the count Trim, the largest castle and the most spectacular rectangular keep in Ireland. The castle established there by Hugh de Lacy very early in the 1170s was a ringwork with strong wooden palisades, and the work of transforming this into a stone castle began early in John's reign. Part of the curtain wall, with rectangular towers and an impressive square-built gatehouse, were being constructed; inside the enceinte a stone platform was built, and a large keep had been started, but not completed, by 1210. The keep was finished in the 1220s and subsequently underwent a number of changes, with rectangular additions to three faces. At the same time the curtain wall was completed; the mural towers are D-shaped, but there are indications that some of them were originally intended to be completely circular. Later still, about 1250, a large circular tower was added as a second gatehouse, protected by two drawbridges and a barbican. The result is a curious mixture of archaic and modern features.

It is odd that rectangular keeps already distinctly old-fashioned in England, though not to the same extent in Wales, should have been used for these Irish castles of the thirteenth century. The explanation is a matter of conjecture, but three factors may be relevant. They may have been simpler to build, especially if much of the work-force was drawn from the local area. Then again, so many of the Anglo-Norman settlers were men from lesser baronial families with experience of an older type of castle: Manorbier, from which Gerald of Wales and his brothers came, is a case in point. A third possibility is that the old-style keep provided more space for a hall and living quarters for the lord and his household without the need to build a separate hall and kitchens within the bailey.

More up-to-date styles were to be found. Remnants of a polygonal keep have survived at Shanid. At Athlone John de Gray, justiciar between 1208 and 1212, built a polygonal keep as the core of a new castle to guard the river-crossing. Much later an outer defence of curtain wall and drum towers was added. Two major circular keeps have survived: at Dundrum John de Courcy fortified the site with a strong curtain wall in the 1180s, and by 1211 he had added a large circular keep as the principal feature of the castle. At Nenagh Theobald Walter replaced his early castle with a stone fortress, building a large circular keep and a strong five-sided curtain wall. While the outer works have disappeared, the keep survives, partly because in the nineteenth century a local bishop rebuilt the top storey in a style that can only be described as fanciful Norman.

There is a group of castles in Leinster associated especially with William Marshal and his sons. They are similar in style and design and are marked by round towers linked by high curtain walling. The remains at Carlow, which may be the earliest of the sequence, suggest a large keep, while Ferns – technically regarded as a keep –

and Kilkenny each presents a strongly fortified enclosure. At Ferns one corner tower is built on a larger scale than the others and served as a principal residence. Work on Kilkenny has been dated to the first decade of the thirteenth century. Here a large circular keep and two smaller circular towers remain from William Marshal's castle. As with Arundel and Warwick, the castle survived and was adapted as a great house and used as their principal seat by the Butlers until 1973; massive changes and rebuildings have obscured the original shape and layout of the enceinte.

The similarities between these strongholds owe much to two factors. The first is that William Marshal's full impact on his Irish lordship was delayed until at least 1204, and he may not himself have been in Ireland earlier than 1208. The second is that by that time he had spent nineteen years improving and extending his Welsh castles, and what he achieved in Ireland was much influenced by that long, earlier experience. After his death in 1219 his sons – and especially his eldest son William, who held his lordships from 1219 to 1231 – continued his building programme. This can first be seen in Wales, at Chepstow, where a new building was begun, soon after William Marshal's death in 1219, as a dower residence for his widow. That led to the completion of a new bailey on the cliff top, and that in turn was followed by more elaborate extensions towards the town and the river bank. It is clear that the architects or master masons responsible for work at Chepstow were also influential (if not personally involved) in Leinster. Window mouldings at Ferns are similar to windows in the early thirteenth-century work at Chepstow, and arrow slits there, and perhaps at Carlow, are closely similar to those at Chepstow, which have been dated 1219–45.

The achievements of de Courcy, Lacy and Marshal were matched by the crown at Dublin (see pp. 111, 113) and at Limerick. Here the castle guarding the river crossing was captured and slighted in 1203, and the opportunity was taken to build an enceinte with no keep. The new castle was still demanding heavy investment in 1212 when £733 16s 11d was paid for works on this site. King John's castle was a five-sided enclosure with corner towers, one of which was rebuilt on a larger scale in the seventeenth century, and with a gatehouse which has the hallmark of later work. The riverside frontage is still very impressive, but the interior of the castle has been sadly gutted.

Ecclesiastical Architecture

From the middle of the eleventh century the Romanesque style, introduced from Normandy, became the dominant style for English churches, large and small, but the general pattern was adapted to meet a wide variety of demands. Function determined the scale of the building and the use of space within the building. In small parish churches local clerics were responsible for their communities and for teaching them the basic elements of belief. Domesday Book points to but understates the extent to which this pattern had developed before the end of the Conqueror's reign. The elaborate decoration of chancel arches, such as that at Elkstone, and of doorways, such as that at Windrush, suggests churches valued by the local lord and his people. Changes in monastic discipline and the introduction of lay brothers (*conversi*) made changes necessary in the internal arrangement of large monastic churches. The cult of saints, with their shrines as centres of devotion and healing, was maintained and increased and, again, demanded great changes in the use of those churches that housed popular shrines.

Death and the fear of what lay beyond death were ever present features of life. It was held that death must be followed by a period of suffering, whether as cleansing or as punishment; prayer and pious works by the living might bring amelioration to those in torment. Beyond that lay the expectation of a Last Judgement, when those who were accepted would pass to eternal bliss, and those rejected to eternal torment. A tombstone at Ely, normally assumed to be that of Bishop Nigel, who died in 1169, reflects the height of ambition and hope; St Michael carries the soul of the dead man to heaven free from fear and secure in the angel's keeping. But, in general, fear – not hope – was the dominant emotion. A high mortality rate, especially for the newly born, for children and for a military elite often actively engaged in conflict, made such fears an unavoidable part of family life. Charters recording gifts to monasteries, cathedrals and parish churches emphasize over and over again that the donors were making their gifts for the safety of the souls of their kindred. In return for their patronage they required the prayers of the religious community, and especially they desired masses to be said for themselves and their immediate family. One result of this, especially in monastic churches, was the need for many altars in subsidiary chapels where such masses could be offered. There was, too, an increasing need for monks to be ordained to the priesthood to celebrate the mass.

Fear of torment was in itself a deterrent to wrongdoing; paintings of judgement, of the reward of the virtuous in bliss and of the punishment of the wicked were to be found in many churches. Early examples have often been replaced in later centuries or destroyed in the religious conflicts of later ages. Between about 1130 and 1140 the chapel of St Gabriel in the crypt which Prior Ernulf built at Canterbury Cathedral was decorated with an elaborate scheme of paintings showing Christ in glory, surrounded by the blessed. In the same period at Kempley, a small parish church in Gloucestershire, the chancel was used to demonstrate the glories of heaven. One large parish church at Clayton in Sussex still has impressive remains of a Last Judgement painted about 1150; Christ is depicted in glory, with St Peter and St Paul, and the paintings of those who have been taken into heaven have survived. The parallel sequence showing those who have been consigned to hell has been severely damaged. But a vivid example of that has survived in the parish church of Chaldon in Surrey, where Christ is seen releasing souls from the torments of hell, the artists giving full scope to the horrors being endured by the damned.

For an illiterate age, such visual aids were an important source of religious teaching. They very often imposed a distorted view of medieval theology. The temptation, then as throughout the medieval period, was to concentrate on the wicked and their fate and to give too much emphasis to punishment. It was much more difficult to suggest (whether in paintings or sculptures) the subtleties of forgiveness and compassion. Even so, artists did not avoid more difficult subjects. Scenes from the lives of the Virgin Mary (at Hardham), of St John (at Guildford) and of St Cuthbert (at Pittington) provided clear teaching from the New Testament and from people of exemplary lives. Carvings on capitals and fonts could do the same. The story of Adam and Eve was popular: at Hook Norton a crude carving, by a local craftsman, stands in sharp contrast with a finely worked series of scenes from their story at East Meon. The judgement of Solomon (at Westminster Abbey), the miraculous draft of fishes (at Lewes Priory) and Jesus with his disciples on the lake (at Much Wenlock) could stand for many sculptured scenes to be found in England in the twelfth century.

With some of the larger churches, links with continental work can be established, and even in small churches in comparatively remote areas such links existed. At Brinsop in Herefordshire a carved relief of St George and the dragon is based on a similar sculpture at Parthenay-le-Vieux, not far from Poitiers. Another Herefordshire church, Fownhope, has a beautifully carved tympanum, with a seated figure holding a child. At first sight it could be a carving of the Virgin Mary with the infant Jesus on her lap. But some details suggest that it represents an image of the godhead, with God the Father holding Christ. By any standard, that would be a very sophisticated image to find in a simple country church. The critical amalgam of an informed patron, a gifted artist and perhaps a cleric with a clear idea of the teaching he hoped to leave with his people can rarely be identified, though it must explain many of the visual aids used in parish churches.

Not all the imagery of the twelfth-century artists can be interpreted with certainty. At Kempley, with the religious images which were their main concern, the artists have painted two bishops and two laymen dressed as pilgrims. Who they are and why they are there are matters of conjecture. The Lacy family held Kempley, and it has been suggested that the two laymen represent early members of that Norman family. Paintings in the Shropshire parish of Claverley, dating from about 1200, have a more sophisticated theme and depict a series of battles between virtues and vices. Quite apart from their religious purpose, they show single combats between a number of fully armed mounted knights, with chainmail, surcoats, conical helmets with protective nose-pieces, swords, lances and shields. Just so might they have appeared in the lists in a tournament, or in battle. They have much in common with the carvings on the twelfth-century font at Southrop, though here the figures combating the vices are not knights, but armed women. The classical imagery and the style of carving seem to owe much to French influence.

Until the end of the eleventh century the Benedictine order offered the only pattern for a regular community life. A body of professed monks accepted a rule of life, and their monastery was organized so that they could maintain their round of worship in the monastic church and organize the economic life of their community and its estates. They might have a large body of servants and attendants who would need living quarters within the enclave, but these were not men living under religious discipline. Other communities, secular clergy living a communal life in a cathedral such as Lincoln or a minster church such as Beverley, maintained a similar pattern.

The foundation of the Cistercian order introduced a major change. To release themselves from the secular demands of their monastic life they added to their number lay brothers (*conversi*) who would be responsible for the practical work of running their estates, and who were themselves living under religious discipline. They used the nave of their monastic church to keep some of the daily offices. The monastic choir had to be separated from the nave by a heavy stone screen (the *pulpitum*), and the lay brothers had to be housed, usually in the western range of the conventual buildings, and to have direct access to the nave. Two communities could, in those conditions, maintain their different patterns of religious observance, though sometimes at the expense of creating very large establishments. In Yorkshire, Byland had 36 monks and 100 lay brothers, and Rievaulx 140 monks and 500 lay brothers, while at Fountains the abbey built accommodation for 200 lay brothers. In Wales, Margam Abbey had 38 monks and 40 lay brothers. It is hardly surprising that at Rievaulx and Margam the order had to deal with social problems and internal unrest.

A number of churches attracted many pilgrims to the shrines of their saints. Norman bishops fostered the cult of St Cuthbert at

Durham and St Swithun at Winchester. Other Anglo-Saxon saints continued to be honoured; among them the cults of two Anglo-Saxon martyr kings remained popular, Edmund of East Anglia (841–69) at Bury, which soon became Bury St Edmunds, and Edward, who ruled England briefly from 975 to 978, at the nunnery of Shaftesbury. After the Conquest local cults multiplied. To cite only three examples, cults developed at Worcester, at the tomb of Bishop Wulfstan, who died in 1095, at Lincoln at the tomb of Bishop Hugh, who died in 1200, and at Norwich at the tomb of a young boy, William, said to have been murdered by the Jews. At Much Wenlock the tomb of St Milburga was opened and found to be empty but, whether through wishful thinking or pious inspiration, the monks were led to find what they believed to be her body and to restore it to its rightful place. In each case pilgrims sought healing and found cures and the shrine became a source of profit for the church. At Melrose, where miracles were said to have occurred at the grave of Abbot Waldef, his successor alienated his monks by failing to recognize the potential value of such a shrine. Annoyed at the disturbance to the peace of his abbey, he refused to move quickly, and the opportunity to build up a cult was lost.

Two national cults developed in England after the Conquest. At Westminster Abbey Edward the Confessor's shrine became a place of pilgrimage, but by far the most spectacular cult of the twelfth century was that of Thomas Becket at Canterbury. Murdered in 1170, he was canonized in 1173, and shrewd publicists at the cathedral built up the reputation of his shrine, almost as a modern business manager may build up the reputation of his firm. The pilgrimage to Canterbury became widely popular in the twelfth century and remained so throughout the later middle ages. Cures were recorded meticulously and systematically, and the cathedral grew rich from the offerings of the pilgrims. Churches on recognized pilgrim routes also prospered as staging posts on the roads to Canterbury.

For monks and canons, the influx of pilgrims necessitated great changes in the use of their churches. They had to ensure that pilgrims could move easily and reach the shrine, which became the focal point of the church. At St David's pilgrims could process around the outside of the church and see the shrine of the saint through an opening in the east wall. Later the east end was extended and the shrine could be approached from within. In 1275, in yet another change, a new shrine was built on the north side of the presbytery in an attempt to allow pilgrims to move more effectively. At Canterbury, anticipating future demand, a new east end was built to house Becket's shrine, and the long processional route through the nave and up the pilgrims' stairs, worn down by the tread of many feet, saw many thousands of supplicants pass through the church to the shrine itself.

For secular cathedrals like York and Salisbury, or for Benedictine monasteries like Bury St Edmunds, a large influx of visitors and sightseers did not produce insuperable problems. At Durham, as at St David's, a more elaborate eastern arm was added to the church, partly to accommodate pilgrims and partly to reduce inconvenience for those seeking to maintain a regular pattern of worship. In monasteries that had adopted the stricter regime of the Cistercians the difficulties were much greater. For much of the twelfth century the building of tombs in Cistercian churches was severely limited, and those that were permitted had to be very simple. When William, first abbot of Rievaulx, died in 1145, he was buried in the chapter house; he was regarded as a saint and revered by his Cistercian associates, but there was no elaborate tomb to act as a focus for his cult. This early severity remained strong until the death of Bernard of Clairvaux in 1153. Only in the thirteenth century was this discipline relaxed and major tombs allowed in the order's continental houses. Even then, only men could enter their churches and penetrate to a shrine; women were excluded. That problem and its solution were made plain comparatively late in the thirteenth century. At Pontigny an English archbishop, Edmund Rich, was buried and later canonized, and his tomb became a centre of pilgrimage. In 1249, when his remains were transferred to a more ornate chest (technically a feretory), one arm was encased in a separate reliquary so that it could be carried outside the church for the benefit of women who were making the pilgrimage to his tomb. Later still, in 1270, the Cistercians at Hailes Abbey were given a phial containing liquid said to be the blood of Christ, and to make that relic easily available they built a new eastern arm to their abbey so that pilgrims could visit it freely without entering or disturbing the monastic area of the church.

The first Romanesque church in England was Edward the Confessor's new building for the abbey of Westminster. His scheme was inaugurated about 1050, when the king was very much under the influence of his Norman archbishop of Canterbury, Robert of Jumièges. Robert had been abbot of Jumièges since 1040, and in his early years he was responsible for building a new eastern end for the abbey church there. His appointment as bishop of London in 1044 and archbishop of Canterbury in 1051 made him a powerful figure in English politics, but when he was driven out of the English kingdom in 1052, he returned to Jumièges and remained abbot there until 1067. We know that in 1052 the new nave there had not been started, though the plans for the new abbey were probably linked with the foundations of the building it replaced, and a large new west work may already have been built earlier in the century. Within those limits, his work at Jumièges was much influenced by what had been planned for Westminster, and the ruined nave at Jumièges may give a fair impression of the Confessor's abbey. Edward's church was rebuilt in a new style in the thirteenth century, and only fragments of Norman work survive in the monastic buildings.

At Canterbury the cathedral was badly damaged by fire in 1067, and soon after his appointment Archbishop Lanfranc had to build a new church in the Norman style. In Normandy he already had considerable experience as a church-builder. At Bec he was the abbot's right-hand man when work on a new abbey began about 1060; that took thirteen years to complete, and Lanfranc was there for the vital planning stages. In 1063 he was appointed abbot of the newly founded abbey of St Stephen's at Caen, and his first task was to build an abbey church. The influence of his work there spread widely in Normandy and England. His new cathedral, built between 1070 and 1077, owed much to Caen, but Lanfranc was already aware of technical changes that could improve Canterbury, which was no mere copy. The cathedral was developed and expanded after Lanfranc's death. Under his successor, Anselm, and two active priors, Ernulf and Conrad, the east end was extended, with a splendid crypt supporting an enlarged choir. A late and practical Norman addition, which still survives, was a water tower built by Prior Wibert in 1160. In 1174 the choir was destroyed by fire and Norman work was replaced by a graceful French Gothic choir. With rebuilding in the nave, the central tower and the Norman west front, almost the whole of Lanfranc's work was replaced. One of his western towers survived until 1834, when that too was demolished. Today it requires an expert eye to identify fragments of his original church.

A third great church where only fragments of Norman work are still visible is the cathedral at Winchester. The Norman bishop, Walkelin, had been a canon of Rouen and was well aware of contemporary developments in Norman architecture, but at Winchester he planned a very large cathedral with some elements more in keeping with contemporary German architecture. He planned at least six towers, one over the central crossing, one at each corner of the transepts, and either a tower at the west end of the nave or two flanking towers as part of an extensive west work. In 1107, nine years after the cathedral was finished, the central tower collapsed and a great deal of rebuilding was necessary. At the end of the fourteenth century the nave was remodelled and Norman pillars were used as the core of the elaborate piers of the new nave. Outwardly the nave retained no vestige of Norman work, but the general proportions and ground-plan of the building followed the Norman scheme very closely. Happily, the north transept was never modernized, and the early Norman work surviving there points to the design of Walkelin's cathedral and to the style of arcading employed there.

Westminster, Canterbury and Winchester (together with the ruins of St Augustine's Abbey at Canterbury) suggest one important difference between the greater Romanesque churches of Normandy and England. In England the churches were very long; the nave of Westminster Abbey had twelve bays and Winchester thirteen; Jumièges and Caen had eight. At Westminster the new abbey was built to the east of the old, and the nave could only be completed when the old church had been demolished. Winchester was built across the line of the Anglo-Saxon cathedral and, again, the nave could not be completed until the old church had been abandoned and demolished. At Canterbury Lanfranc demolished the remains of the existing cathedral to the foundations before laying out his new church. In these circumstances the architects could work without constraints. St Augustine's is a reminder that the design of the east end could be elaborate. The eleventh-century foundations point to an ambulatory with three radiating chapels. Lewes Priory, built before the end of the century, had five chapels.

The Romanesque church depended upon the use of arcades of rounded arches. The main and most impressive arcade would be surmounted by a second stage – the triforium or the tribune – and that in turn carried the clerestory where the wall could be pierced for windows. Architects were skilful in varying the proportions of these storeys; the triforium could be decorated with the use of a central pillar and a double arch, as at Chichester, or a triple arch, as at Jumièges. St Albans Abbey, where building started in 1077, has a more complex pattern of four pillars carrying narrow open arcading surmounted by blind arcades thrown from the middle pillar to the two outer pillars. The same pattern, with more ornate decoration, is to be found at St Peter's Abbey in Gloucester, now the cathedral, where building started twelve years later. The windows of the clerestory can vary between simple, unadorned embrasures to more elaborate combinations of pillars and arcades. Above the triforium a lean-to roof provides cover for strong buttresses supporting the height of the nave or, where they survive in Norman form, the chancel. Blind arcading, with pillar and arch constructed against a blank wall, was a popular form of decoration. Of many possible examples, the nave of Gloucester Cathedral (1089–1100), the chapter house at Worcester Cathedral (before 1125) and the chapter house at St Augustine's Abbey at Bristol, now the cathedral (*c*.1150–70), may serve to illustrate this feature.

While arcades provided a strong horizontal line, the height of the greater churches made possible a striking vertical emphasis by the use of tall shafts running the full height of the wall. At Ely and Peterborough, for example, they are placed at each pillar and give an increased impression of great height. At Westminster and Jumièges, and many derivative churches, they are found on alternate pillars, and the bays are arranged in pairs. Where, as at Durham, circular pillars alternate with compound piers, horizontal and vertical patterns present a striking whole.

Structural purity was combined with a rich variety of decoration. Mouldings of arches, doors and windows were designed with patterns of chevron, dog-tooth, lozenge and beak-head, sometimes with a single motif repeated in profusion, as beak-head decoration is used on the west front of Iffley church, and sometimes, as at Malmesbury, with different motifs used for successive mouldings. The tympanum, filling an arch above an inset door, gave great opportunities for artistic imagination. Capitals, providing a firm platform between pillar and wall, produced a wide range of design, from simple cushion shape to ornate spiral designs or to vivid sculptures of biblical scenes and incidents from the cults of many saints.

It was a characteristic of Norman Romanesque building that it did not produce the great richness of sculpture and capitals so typical of central and southern France. One consequence is that decorative art in churches in the British Isles owed much to native traditions; Canterbury and Winchester had a long tradition of manuscript illumination which influenced the style of much post-conquest sculpture. Local traditions left their mark on many churches. The sculptured decoration of Kilpeck church and a strong Herefordshire school of intricate scroll and figure work represent one important local tradition. The high quality of twelfth-century work at St Mary's Abbey, York, may be another example. In Ireland, the combination of qualities of Irish and Romanesque elements produced a unique style.

Each great Norman church is a distinct entity, but many display similarities that sometimes suggest uniformity. That is due in part to the fact that each building is a variation on a common style. But it may owe much to the fact that stone from particular areas was much valued and imported for prestigious buildings. To import and cut stone from the quarries near Caen, for example, was costly; it was more economical to buy stone already cut at the quarry. The result was the use of similar, if not identical, patterns in different buildings. For that reason, it is particularly instructive to examine styles and motifs used in churches built from local stone. The Norman work at Worcester Cathedral was built from limestone from the Cotswolds, and it is not surprising to find that some of the decorative motifs used in the nave in the 1180s are unique in the area at that date.

To see a complete Norman church untouched by later work it is useful to look at the chapels of the earliest great stone keeps; the eleventh-century chapel in the Tower of London and the chapel built about a hundred years later in the keep at Dover present the Romanesque church in miniature. So, in Scotland, does the chapel of Edinburgh castle with its simple nave and apse divided by an ornate chancel arch. The crypt chapel in Durham castle was much damaged by later alterations and with judicious rebuilding has been carefully restored. For a large-scale church, Norwich has a remarkable unity. The choir and apse were built between 1096 and 1120, and the nave had been completed by 1145. A disastrous fire, the collapse of the central tower and subsequent repair and rebuilding did not alter the basic structure of the Romanesque church. Despite long delays in building, Peterborough has a similar unity. Work on a new church was started in 1118, and over the next twenty-five years the eastern end was completed. It was not until the last quarter of the twelfth century that the nave was built, but then, by a deliberate decision, it was built in the same style as the rest of the church.

At Durham Cathedral the Norman east end was demolished and replaced in the thirteenth century, but the greater part of the cathedral built between 1096 and 1128 is intact. The nave arcading, richly decorated, consists of alternate pillars and compound piers made up of clusters of small shafts; the pillars have been decorated with distinctive incised patterns. The nave was given a vaulted roof between 1128 and 1133, and Durham escapes the contrast, so often to be seen in Norman churches, of a Romanesque shell matched with a later roof, beautiful in its own right but inappropriate in its setting. Durham has important links with the Romanesque abbey church built at Dunfermline. Excavation has shown that a Romanesque east end had been added to the small church which served the priory there, but this was replaced when, in 1128, the priory was made an abbey. The nave is a mixture of primitive and sophisticated elements. The triforium is very simple in design and suggests an early date. The pillars and the main arcading have much in common with Durham Cathedral. The assumption must be that masons finishing their work at Durham in 1128 moved north and built the abbey church at Dunfermline.

The classic Norman west front, characteristic of so many churches in the duchy, can be seen in St Stephen's Abbey at Caen. The gable of the nave is framed by towers which are functional as well as decorative; the west front is restrained and austere, with a simple pattern of windows and decoration limited to the three storeys of the towers. (Thirteenth-century spires reflect the taste of a later age.) In England, the west front at Durham retains a great deal of twelfth-century work, and at Southwell minster, where the western end of the nave was completed between 1120 and 1130, the classic form is preserved. The twin towers have a minimum of decoration and only a large fifteenth-century window breaks the rhythm of the Norman façade. The interior is beautifully proportioned and sophisticated in design.

The west midlands produced a local style of Romanesque building. At Gloucester Abbey Abbot Serlo began to build a new church in 1089. The eastern end was designed in orthodox fashion with a main arcade and a spacious triforium which gave access to radiating chapels; this part of the church and, presumably, the transepts were consecrated in 1100, and in the four years before he died Serlo began to build the nave. The planning of the whole church, in principle if not in detail, was his work. For the nave he used large cylindrical pillars which carried an arcade of narrow arches to the height of the normal triforium; it is known, as a matter of convenience, as giant order. This style was derived from the Burgundian abbey at Tournus. Above the arcade he planned a much reduced triforium, designed almost as a decorative feature, and a clerestory (much altered in later rebuilding). The two western bays of the nave were built before Serlo's death, and the nave was completed by his immediate successors by about 1120. A disastrous fire damaged the nave in 1121, and the building record for the rest of the century is obscure.

The same style was used at Tewkesbury Abbey, and it occurs at Hereford and Pershore. When, at a later date, Gloucester and Tewkesbury were refashioned, the Norman work was not demolished, and behind the later remodelling the framework of the Romanesque nave and eastern apse in each church is virtually complete.

Notable examples of Romanesque work are to be found in Wales, often in small parish churches. Only fragments of Norman work survive at Llandaff Cathedral to suggest the scale of the church built in the twelfth century, but there are very extensive Norman elements at St David's, where Bishop Peter de Leia (1176–98) built a new cathedral. The six bays of the nave, with richly decorated arcading, are the most impressive surviving feature, while the triforium, again richly decorated, has also been used to provide the main windows for the nave. The cathedral was extensively and sympathetically restored by Scott in the nineteenth century.

Small Benedictine priories produced attractive Norman architecture. Chepstow Priory church has a classical Romanesque west front, with two well-designed buttresses and a fine doorway framed by blind arcades and surmounted by a triple window. Norman work dominates the interior. Ewenni was a small cruciform church built before 1134 and extended after it was given the status of a priory in 1141; the nave (with a north aisle added late in the twelfth century), transepts, a rectangular chancel and a central tower all survive. A small but very beautiful Norman church at Newport was for many centuries the parish church of St Woolos, which became the cathedral church of the diocese of Monmouth in 1920. At the west end is a small building, older in date than the church, now known as the chapel of St Mary. That should be the church that was given to Gloucester Abbey between 1087 and 1099; the present St Woolos was presumably commissioned by the monks between 1107 and 1147 under the patronage of Robert, earl of Gloucester. The nave is based on arcades of simple pillars, and in place of a triforium there are simple window embrasures. From the chapel an ornate Norman arch gives access to the nave, and the chapel serves – as if it were a narthex – as an extended entry for the church itself. When new aisles were built in the fifteenth century and additions made in the nineteenth and twentieth centuries, the nave and its chapel were not disturbed.

For the most part, churches built by the new monastic orders in Wales (as in Scotland) survive as ruins. Although the greater part of Margam Abbey has disappeared, the nave survives as the parish church. Neath, Valle Crucis and Basingwerk suggest the scale of building by the Cistercians and their close counterparts at Savigny; Llanthony, impressive in its isolated site, was an influential Augustinian house. Talley, with the signs that it was never completed, suggests the isolation of this single Welsh house of the Premonstratensian order.

In Scotland St Andrews presents an interesting sequence. There is the shrine church of St Regulus, which has the appearance of an Anglo-Saxon church. A high tower was built as a landmark, and in style and detail it strongly resembles the early twelfth-century church at Wharram-le-Street. Nostell priory provides a link between the two churches, and it seems clear that masons who had worked at Wharram-le-Street moved on to work at St Regulus' church. The ruins of the cathedral include a Romanesque east end of about 1200. The high tower of St Regulus has parallels in churches built later in the century in Perthshire and Fife. Two exceptionally fine parish churches survive from the mid-twelfth century. Dalmeny, closely associated with the family of Earl Cospatric, is largely complete, with an elaborate south door surmounted by blind arcading. At Leuchars the east end of the Romanesque church survives, the chancel and apse decorated with bold confidence with two tiers of blind arcading. Both churches have links with the abbey church at Dunfermline; masons' marks indicate that the same masons were at work on all three churches. Premonstratensian canons were established by Hugh of Morville at Dryburgh in 1150, where extensive remains of Romanesque work survive in the transepts and the cloister. Of the Augustinian houses in Scotland the ruins of Jedburgh Abbey are the most extensive and impressive. Unexpectedly, the builders made dramatic use of giant order pillars in the choir.

For Romanesque architecture in Ireland Cormac's chapel, built at Cashel between 1127 and 1134, is a building of seminal importance. Under the patronage of Cormac Mac Carthy a Benedictine priory was established there and, since a kinsman of the king was a monk at Regensburg, the abbot sent two Irish monks and two craftsmen to Cashel some time between 1121 and 1133 to further this project. The exterior, and especially the south wall of the nave, was decorated with an elaborate pattern of blind arcading rising in four vertical bands. Similar blind arcading occurs on the tower and the chancel wall, though decoration here was used with great economy. The north and south doors, each with a tympanum, are richly decorated, and the north door has an elaborate gable. The interior of the chapel has a well-organized scheme incorporating windows, short pillars and blind arcading. The chapel clearly owes something to contemporary work in German churches, and especially to Regensburg. Unfortunately, much of the early work at Regensburg has been lost in rebuilding and the derivation cannot be identified in detail. When the chapel of All Saints at Regensburg was being built in the 1160s, a pattern of blank arcading was still being used, but the work was done by Lombard masons, and whether they followed earlier practice at the abbey or imported their own scheme cannot be determined.

Cormac's chapel has been seen, quite properly, as an influential building in the development of early Irish Romanesque architecture, and the sources from which those who built the chapel drew their inspiration continue to be the subject of conjecture and debate. The exterior of the twelfth-century cathedral at Ardfert (now to be judged only by fragments preserved and reused in the thirteenth century) and the interior of the nave of Kilmalkedar church echo themes found at Cashel. The decorated gable of the north door at Cashel must be the major influence on the development of this feature of Irish Romanesque churches. It was combined with a characteristic pitch of the lintels of church doors, which were set, not upright, but at an angle. The gable, flanked by blind arcading, which survives from the twelfth-century church at Roscrea, is more austere than anything at Cashel. The Romanesque church at

Clonfert has Romanesque east windows with quite sophisticated mouldings, and it is no surprise to find that it also has a very fine west door. The original had six orders of moulding, all set at an angle, and the seventh order, added in the fifteenth century and set upright, serves to emphasize the balance of the earlier work. Each moulding of the arch has a different pattern of decoration, and the gable has an intricate design of blind arcading surmounted by a pattern of triangular masks.

Foundations reveal the scale of the twelfth-century church at Mellifont, source of so much Cisterican expansion in Ireland, and the ruins of an octagonal lavabo indicate the quality of its early buildings. The abbey that demonstrates most clearly the development of monastic church architecture in Ireland is Jerpoint. About 1160 a Benedictine abbey was founded there under the patronage of the king of Ossory, and some fragments of early building survive in the east wall of the chancel and the transepts. The monks planned a cruciform church with an aisle-less nave. The house did not flourish; in 1180 it was colonized by Cistercians from Baltinglass, and the church was extended and completed. The nave was redesigned with north and south arcades, side aisles, cloisters and conventual buildings. The church was given a large western tower, which may have been built partly for prestige. The abbey was associated with a grange and a settlement – Newtown Jerpoint – founded at the turn of the century by a prominent Anglo-Norman settler, perhaps Griffin fitz William or Earl William Marshal (Barry, 1987). The abbey attracted settlement, which in turn appears to have influenced the scale of the church.

Baltinglass was itself one of a number of colonies established by Mellifont in the 1140s, which included Bective, Boyle and Monasteranenagh. Of these, the remains of the abbey at Boyle are the most impressive. Founded in 1161, the progress of the building can be traced through the south arcade, completed about 1180, and the north arcade, built between 1190 and 1200. The Romanesque work carried out over forty years extends from the east end, through the transepts and nave to the simple west front. Windows inserted in the north wall are a rare indication of later work. The explanation seems to be that the planning of the church was influenced by one of the order's Burgundian monasteries and perhaps by the presence of a master mason who had worked in Dublin. But it is clear that local craftsmen were active on the site. R. A. Stalley (1971) noted that the quality of worked stone at Boyle and at least four other churches pointed to one sculptor, and perhaps a group of men, working under local patronage. He also cited the death in 1230 of 'a holy monk and chief master of the carpenters', Donnsleibhe Ohlnmhainen'. Boyle Abbey brings us closer than other Irish churches to the individuals who helped to plan and build them.

Between 1050 and 1200, kings, magnates, clerics and administrators appear in records and chronicles; they can be identified and seen as personalities. Builders and artists are almost always anonymous. A small minority, like Gundulf of Rochester, Maurice the king's architect, and Donnsleibhe may be identified. The rest can be known only from their surviving achievements.

Outline Chronologies

Rulers of England

Edward the Confessor	1042–66
Harold	January–October 1066
William I	1066–87
William II (Rufus)	1087–1100
Henry I	1100–35
Stephen	1135–54
Henry II	1154–89
Richard I	1189–99
John	1199–1216
Henry III	1216–72

Rulers of Scotland

Macbeth	1040–57
Lulach	1057–8
Malcolm III (Canmore)	1058–93
Donald Bàn	1093–7 (with a brief interregnum, May–November 1094, when Duncan II reigned)
Edgar	1093/7–1107 (Edgar was a claimant

	from 1093, acknowledged by William Rufus from 1095.)
Alexander I	1107–24
David I	1124–53
Malcolm IV (the Maiden)	1153–65
William I (the Lion)	1165–1214
Alexander II	1214–49

Rulers in Wales

The succession is often broken. For some of the lesser kingdoms, only rulers mentioned in the text are named here.

Gwynedd

Gruffydd ap Llywelyn	1039–63
Bleddyn ap Cynfyn	1063–75
Trahaearn ap Caradog	1075–81
Gruffydd ap Cynan	1081–1137
Owain Gwynedd	1137–70
Cynan ab Owain	1170–4 (after an interregnum in parts of the kingdom)
Llywelyn ab Iorwerth	1195–1240 (in control of the whole of Gwynedd from 1202)

Powys

Gruffydd ap Llywelyn	1039–63
Rhiwallon ap Cynfyn	1063–70
Bleddyn ap Cynfyn	1070–5

Thereafter, for two generations, brothers shared or contested power in different parts of Powys. Of these, Cadwgan ap Bleddyn (d.1111) and Maredudd ap Bleddyn (d.1132) were the most prominent rulers.

Madog ap Maredudd   1132–60
Thereafter, the principality was divided between five
claimants.

Deheubarth

Hywel ab Edwin   1035–44 (Hywel shared authority
                                                    with his brother, Maredudd, from
                                                    1033 to 1035.)
Gruffydd ap Rhydderch   1044–55
Gruffydd ap Llywelyn   1055–63
Maredudd ab Owain   *c*.1063–72
Rhys ab Owain   1072–8
Rhys ap Tewdwr   1078–93
[Gruffydd ap Rhys ap Tewdwr]

There was a long interregnum between 1093 and 1137.
Gruffydd ap Rhys ap Tewdwr, claimant to Deheubarth, spent
many years in exile in Ireland, sought to gain power by
military action and received only a small patrimony. He
preserved his dynasty's claims to the kingdom, and Welsh
annalists described him in terms appropriate for an acknowledged prince. Between 1137 and 1155 his four sons worked
closely together, and each was acknowledged as prince of
Deheubarth.

Anarawd ap Gruffydd   1137–43
Cadell ap Gruffydd   1143–*c*.1153 (Cadell was seriously
                                                    wounded in 1151. He was
                                                    nominally in power when he went
                                                    on pilgrimage to Rome in 1153 and
                                                    left the kingdom in the care of his
                                                    younger brothers. He later became
                                                    a monk at Strata Florida; he died
                                                    in 1175.)
Maredudd ap Gruffydd   *c*.1153–5
Rhys ap Gruffydd   1155–97

Gwynllŵg

Gruffydd ap Rhydderch	1033–55
Caradog ap Gruffydd	1055–81
Morgan ab Owain (grandson of Caradog ap Gruffydd)	occurs mid twelfth century

Morgannwg

Caradog ap Gruffydd	d.1081
Iestyn ap Gwrgant	1081 (He was a newcomer, taking over Morgannwg after the death of Caradog ap Gruffydd. After the Normans settled in Morgannwg his family held the lordship of Afan. The date of his death is not known.)

Rulers in Ireland

Aileach

Donal Mac Loughlin	1083–1121
Murchetach Mac Loughlin	1136–43, 1145–66

Bregia

Flanducan	occurs 1028

Bréifne

Tiernan O'Rourke	c.1128–72

Connacht

Turlough O'Connor	1106–56
Rory O'Connor	1156–83
Cathal Crovderg O'Connor	1189–1224

Desmond

Cormac Mac Carthy	1123–38
Dermot Mac Carthy	1143–85

Dublin

Sitric	1000–42
Guthric (Gofraid)	*d*.1075
Asgall	1160–2, 1166–70

Leinster

Dermot Mac Murrough	1126–72

Meath

Art O'Melaghlin	1173–84

Munster

Brian Bóruma	978–1014
Donnchad	1023–64
Turlough O'Brien	1063–86
Murchetach O'Brien	1086–1119

Tyrone

Aedh O'Neill	1196–1230

Ulidia

Rory Mac Dunlevy	1172–1201

The high kings who were powerful during the period of
European and Anglo-Norman impact on Ireland were
Turlough O'Brien, Turlough O'Connor and Rory O'Connor.

Summary of Events

1028	Ireland	Sitric, king of Dublin, and Flanducan, king of Bregia, go on pilgrimage to Rome.
1051	England	Edward the Confessor promises the English throne to Duke William of Normandy.
1055–63	Wales	Gruffydd ap Llywelyn dominant in north and south Wales; attacks Herefordshire and Gloucestershire.
1058–93	Scotland	Reign of Malcolm III; English and Norman influences affect Scottish court.
1063	Wales	Gruffydd ap Llywelyn killed; Welsh princes revert to pattern of local power.
1064	Ireland	Donnchad son of Brian Bóruma goes on pilgrimage to Rome; dies on the journey.
1066	England	Death of Edward the Confessor; accession of Harold; Norwegian invasion; battles of Fulford Gate and Stamford Bridge; Norman invasion of Sussex; battle of Hastings; death of Harold; William the Conqueror crowned.
1066–72	Scotland	Malcolm III receives English rebels in Scotland.
1067–94	Wales	Years of Norman infiltration

		and settlement in Wales: William fitz Osbern in Gwent; Hugh of Avranches and Robert of Rhuddlan in north Wales; Roger of Montgomery in mid and west Wales.
1070–89	England	Lanfranc, archbishop of Canterbury, asserts authority over York; consecrates bishop of Dublin; influences Queen Margaret and the Scottish court.
*c.*1071–2	Scotland	Malcolm III marries Margaret, sister of Edgar the Atheling.
1072	Scotland	William I campaigns in Scotland; Malcolm III acknowledges him as overlord.
1073–85	Ireland	Pope Gregory VII establishes contact with Turlough O'Brien.
1074	Ireland	Archbishop Lanfranc consecrates Patrick as bishop of Dublin.
1078	Wales	Battle of Mynydd Carn; emergence of strong king of south Wales, Rhys ap Tewdwr.
1081	Wales	William I travels to St David's; accord with Rhys ap Tewdwr.
1081–2	Ireland	Archbishop Lanfranc in correspondence with Irish clerics.

1087	England/Wales	Death of William I; renewed infiltration into Wales under William II.
c.1088–90	Wales	Early Norman penetration into Brycheiniog and Morgannwg.
1093	Wales	Death of Rhys ap Tewdwr opens south Wales to Norman expansion.
1094	Ireland	Archbishop Anselm in correspondence with Irish bishops.
1094–8	Wales	Welsh resurgence; recovery of Gwynedd and other territories.
1096	Ireland	Archbishop Anselm consecrates the first bishop of Waterford.
1100	England/Scotland	Henry I marries Matilda, daughter of Malcolm III.
1101	Ireland	Murchetach O'Brien gives Cashel to the church; Council of Cashel.
1102	Wales	Fall of family of Bellême; loss of earldoms of Shrewsbury and Pembroke.
c.1103–35	Wales	Extensive settlement of south Wales under Henry I's patronage.
1107–34	Wales	Urban, bishop of Llandaff, accepts archbishop of Canterbury as metropolitan.
1111	Ireland	Council of Rathbreasil establishes archbishops at Armagh and Cashel.
1113	Scotland	David establishes first Tironensian monastery in

		Scotland at Selkirk; transferred to Kelso, 1128.
1113–24	Scotland	David lord of Annandale and other territories in southern Scotland.
1114	Scotland	David given Maud of St Liz as wife; made earl of Huntingdon.
1114–75	Scotland	A succession of bishops of Glasgow consecrated by Pascal II, Eugenius III and Alexander III.
1124	England	Foundation of first Savigniac abbey in Britain, at Tulketh; transferred to Furness in 1127.
1124–53	Scotland	Reign of David I; period of intensive settlement by Anglo-Norman immigrants.
1124–48	Ireland	Bishop Malachy, patron of monastic expansion.
1127	Ireland	Foundation of first Savigniac abbey in Ireland at Erenagh.
1128	England	Foundation of first Cistercian monastery in Britain, at Waverley.
1131	Wales	Foundation of first Cistercian monastery in Wales at Tintern.
1135–54	Wales	Extensive Welsh resurgence, with heavy Norman losses.
1136	Scotland	Foundation of first Cistercian monastery in Scotland at Melrose.
c.1140–c.1200	Scotland	Slow absorption of Moray.
1142	Ireland	Foundation of first

		Cistercian monastery in Ireland at Mellifont.
1148	Wales	Council of Reims; plan for independent Welsh province lapses.
1152	Ireland	Council of Kells/Mellifont establishes archbishops at Tuam and Dublin.
1155	Ireland	Possible invasion of Ireland by Henry II discussed; papal approval gained.
1155–97	Wales	Reign of Rhys ap Gruffydd; long period of dominance in south Wales.
*c.*1160–*c.*1200	Scotland	Reduction of independence of Galloway.
1166	Ireland	Dermot Mac Murrough ousted from Leinster.
1167–70	Ireland	Strongbow planning and carrying out Irish expedition.
1170	England	Archbishop Thomas Becket murdered in Canterbury Cathedral.
1171–2	Ireland	Henry II's expedition to Ireland; royal claims recognized; Hugh de Lacy given Meath; death of Dermot Mac Murrough.
1172–86	Ireland	Castellation and settlement of Meath.
1173	England	Thomas Becket canonized.
1173–4	England	Rebellion against Henry II throughout his territories.
1174	Scotland	Capture of William the Lion; restored to full power in 1189.

1175	Ireland	Treaty between Henry II and the high king, Rory O'Connor.
1176	Scotland	Tacit recognition of independence of Scottish bishops.
1176	Ireland	Death of Strongbow; intensive castle-building in Leinster by guardians of his young son.
1177	Ireland	Extension of Anglo-Norman settlement into south-west Ireland.
1177–1205	Ireland	John de Courcy invades Ulidia and carves out lordship of Ulster.
1185	Ireland	John, as lord of Ireland, makes formal visit to the lordship; introduces new leading families.
1189	England/Wales	Marriage of William Marshal and Strongbow's heiress creates new power bloc in England and Wales; full impact in Ireland delayed until *c.*1204.
1192	Scotland	Formal recognition of independence of Scottish bishops.
1199–1203	Wales	Gerald of Wales seeks papal judgement in favour of an independent province for Wales but fails.
1207	England	Disgrace of William de Braose breaks power of his family in England, Wales and Ireland.

1210	Ireland	King John campaigns in Ireland; reduces power of Lacy family.
1214–49	Scotland	Late phase of Anglo-Norman/English immigration in reign of Alexander II.
1235	Ireland	Extension of Anglo-Norman infiltration into Connacht.

Architecture

1040–? c.1044	Jumièges Abbey, east end.
1050–65	Westminster Abbey.
1052–67	Jumièges Abbey, nave.
1060–73	Bec Abbey.
1063	St Stephen's, Caen, complete with vaulted roof before 1100.
1067–71	Chepstow, keep in progress.
1070–7	Lanfranc's cathedral at Canterbury.
1070–98	Winchester Cathedral.
1074 or 1076	Colchester keep, perhaps not completed until after 1100.
1077–88	St Albans Abbey.
1078–97	Tower of London, keep.
1089–1121	St Peter's Abbey, Gloucester.
1096–1128	Durham Cathedral, vault complete 1133.
1096–1145	Norwich Cathedral.
1097–9	Westminster hall.
before 1100	Ludlow castle, curtain wall.
1100–35	Norwich castle.
1127–34	Cormac's chapel, Cashel.
1128 or 1133	Dunfermline Abbey.
c.1130–40	Wall paintings in St Gabriel's chapel at

	Canterbury Cathedral, and at Kempley church.
before 1131	Ewenni Priory.
1138	Extensive castle building by William d'Aubigny.
1150	Wall paintings at Clayton church.
1160	First phase of Jerpoint Abbey, with main work after 1181.
1161–*c*.1200	Boyle Abbey.
1168–89	Dover castle, keep.
1175–84	Rebuilding and extension of eastern arm of Canterbury Cathedral after the great fire of 1174; Trinity chapel, built over Becket's tomb, completed by 1179, and the 'corona' at the east end by 1184.
1176–98	St David's Cathedral.
1178–*c*.1228/42	Carrickfergus castle.
1180–89	Dover castle, Henry II's outer defences.
1189–1219	William Marshal's castles in Wales and Ireland.
? late twelfth century	Stone castles in Scotland.
c.1200	Pembroke castle, keep.
c.1200	Wall paintings at the parish churches at Chaldon and Claverley.
c.1200–50	Trim castle, keep complete 1220.

Select Bibliography

This reading list is a small selection from the large number of books and articles that bear on Norman expansion. There are useful and fairly recent bibliographies in Barry 1987, Bartlett 1993, Chibnall 1986, R. R. Davies 1987, Duncan 1975, Flanagan 1989 and Walker 1990.

Altschul, M. 1965: *A Baronial Family in Medieval England: The Clares, 1217–1314*. Baltimore.

Barlow, F. 1955: *The Feudal Kingdom of England 1042–1216*. London. (4th edn 1988.)

Barlow, F. 1963: *The English Church 1000–1066*. London. (2nd edn 1979.)

Barlow, F. 1970: *Edward the Confessor*. London.

Barlow, F. 1979: *The English Church, 1066–1154*. London.

Barlow, F. 1983: *William Rufus*. London. (Paperback edn 1990.)

Barrow, G. W. S. 1956: *Feudal Britain*. London.

Barrow, G. W. S. 1960: *Regesta Regum Scottorum*, I, *Malcolm IV 1153–65*. Edinburgh.

Barrow, G. W. S. 1973: *The Kingdom of the Scots*. London.

Barrow, G. W. S. 1975: 'The pattern of lordship and feudal settlement in Cumbria'. *Journal of Medieval History*, i, 117–38.

Barrow, G. W. S. 1980: *The Anglo-Norman Era in Scottish History*. Oxford.

Barrow, G. W. S. 1981: *Scotland 1000–1306. The New History of Scotland*, vol. 2. London. (New edn 1989.)

Barrow, G. W. S. and Scott, W. W. 1971: *Regesta Regum Scottorum*, II, *William I, 1165–1214*. Edinburgh.

Barry, T. B. 1987: *The Archaeology of Medieval Ireland*. London.

Bartlett, R. 1982: *Gerald of Wales 1146–1223*. Oxford.

Bartlett, R. 1993: *The Making of Europe: Conquest, Colonization and Cultural Change 950–1350*. Harmondsworth.

Bates, D. 1982: *Normandy before 1066*. London.

Bates, D. 1989: *William the Conqueror*. London.

Binchy, D. A. 1970: *Celtic and Anglo-Saxon Kingship*. Oxford.

Boon, G. C. 1986: *Welsh Hoards 1979–81*. Cardiff.

Brett, M. 1970: *The English Church under Henry I*. Oxford.

Brown, R. A. 1981: 'The Battle of Hastings'. *Proceedings of the Battle Conference on Anglo-Norman Studies*, III, 1–21.

Brown, R. A. 1984: *The Normans*. Woodbridge.

Brown, R. A. 1989: *Castles from the Air*. Cambridge.

Byrne, F. J. 1973: *Irish Kings and High-Kings*. London.

Chibnall, M. 1986: *Anglo-Norman England, 1066–1166*. Oxford.

Clarke, H. 1984: *The Archaeology of Medieval England*. London.

Cosgrove, A. (ed.) 1987: *A New History of Ireland*, 2, *Medieval Ireland (1169–1534)*. Oxford. (Revised edn 1993.)

Courtney, P. 1986: 'The Norman invasion of Gwent: a reassessment'. *Journal of Medieval History*, 12, 297–313.

Cowley, F. G. 1977: *The Monastic Order in South Wales 1066–1349*. Cardiff.

Crawford, B. E. 1985: 'The Earldom of Caithness and the Kingdom of Scotland'. In K. Stringer (ed.), *Essays on the Nobility of Medieval Scotland*. Edinburgh, 25–43.

Crouch, D. 1985: 'The slow death of kingship in Glamorgan, 1067–1158'. *Morgannwg*, xxix, 20–41.

Crouch, D. 1986: *The Beaumont Twins*. Cambridge.

Crouch, D. 1988: *Llandaff Episcopal Acta 1140–1287*. Cardiff.

Davies, R. R. 1974: 'Colonial Wales'. *Past and Present*, 65, 3–23.

Davies, R. R. 1978a: *Lordship and Society in the March of Wales 1282–1400*. Oxford.

Davies, R. R. 1978b: 'Brecon'. In R. A. Griffiths (ed.), *Boroughs of Medieval Wales*. Cardiff, 47–70.

Davies, R. R. 1979: 'Kings, lords and liberties in the March of Wales, 1066–1272'. *Transactions of the Royal Historical Society*, 5th series, 29, 41–61.

Davies, R. R. 1985: 'Henry I and Wales'. In H. Mayr-Harting and R. I. Moore (eds), *Studies in Medieval History Presented to R. H. C. Davis*. London, 132–47.

Davies, R. R. 1987: *Conquest, Coexistence and Change: Wales, 1063–1415*. Oxford and Cardiff.

Davies, R. R. 1990: *Domination and Conquest: The Experience of Ireland, Scotland and Wales 1100–1300*. Cambridge.

Davies, W. 1982: *Wales in the Early Middle Ages*. Leicester.

Davis, R. H. C. 1976: *The Normans and their Myth*. London.

Dolley, M. 1972: *Anglo-Norman Ireland*. Dublin.

Douglas, D. C. 1964: *William the Conqueror*. London.

Douglas, D. C. 1969: *The Norman Achievement*. London.

Douglas, D. C. 1976: *The Norman Fate*. London.

Duncan, A. A. M. 1975: *Scotland: The Making of the Kingdom. The Edinburgh History of Scotland*, I. Edinburgh.

Edwards, J. G. 1956: 'The Normans and the Welsh March'. *Proceedings of the British Academy*, xlii, 155–77.

Finucane, R. C. 1977: *Miracles and Pilgrims*. London.

Flanagan, M. T. 1989: *Irish Society, Anglo-Norman Settlers, Angevin Kingship*. Oxford.

Frame, R. 1981: *Colonial Ireland, 1169–1369*. Dublin.

Frame, R. 1982: *English Lordship in Ireland 1318–1361*. Oxford.

Gillingham, J. 1978: *Richard the Lionheart*. London.

Gillingham, J. 1989: 'William the Bastard at war'. In M. Strickland (ed.), *Anglo-Norman Warfare*. Woodbridge, 1992. (Reprinted from C. Harper-Bill, C. Holdsworth and J. Nelson, *Studies in Medieval History Presented to R. Allen Brown*. Woodbridge, 1989.)

Glasscock, R. E. 1975: 'Mottes in Ireland'. *Château-Gaillard*, 7, 95–110.

Graham, B. J. 1985: *Anglo-Norman Settlement in Ireland*. Athlone.

Griffiths, M. 1989: 'Native society on the Anglo-Norman frontier: the evidence of the Margam charters'. *Welsh History Review*, 14, 179–216.

Griffiths, R. A. (ed.) 1978a: *Boroughs of Medieval Wales*. Cardiff.

Griffiths, R. A. 1978b: 'Carmarthen'. In R. A. Griffiths (ed.), *Boroughs of Medieval Wales*. Cardiff, 131–63.

Hollister, C. W. 1986: *Monarchy, Magnates and Institutions in the Anglo-Norman World*. London and Roncerverte. (Includes 'Normandy, France and the Anglo-Norman *regnum*', reprinted from *Speculum*, 51 (1976), 1–25.)

Hollister, C. W. 1987: 'The greater Domesday tenants-in-chief'. In J. C. Holt (ed.), *Domesday Studies*. Woodbridge, 219–48.

Holt, J. C. (ed.) 1987: *Domesday Studies*. Woodbridge.

Kapelle, W. E. 1979: *The Norman Conquest of the North*. London.

Kenyon, J. R. 1990: *Medieval Fortifications*. Leicester. (Paperback edn 1991.)

Kenyon, J. R. and Avent, R. (eds) 1987: *Castles in Wales and the Marches.* Cardiff.

Le Patourel, J. 1969: 'The Norman colonization of Britain'. In *I Normanni e loro espansione in Europa nell' alto medioevo* (papers published by the Centro italiano di studi sull' Alto Medioevo, Spoleto, in *Settimane di Studio*, xvi, 409–38).

Le Patourel, J. 1971: *Normandy and England, 1066–1144.* Reading.

Le Patourel, J. 1976: *The Norman Empire.* Oxford.

Le Patourel, J. 1984: *Feudal Empires: Norman and Plantagenet.* London.

Lennard, R. V. 1959: *Rural England, 1066–1153.* Oxford.

Lewis, C. 1984: 'The Norman settlement of Herefordshire under William I'. *Anglo-Norman Studies*, VII, 195–213.

Lewis, C. 1991: 'The early earls of Norman England'. *Anglo-Norman Studies*, XIII, 207–24.

Lloyd, J. E. 1911: *A History of Wales from the Earliest Times to the Edwardian Conquest.* London. (2 vols, 3rd edn, 1939.)

Martin, F. X. 1987: 'Diarmait Mac Murchada and the coming of the Anglo-Normans', 'Allies and an overlord, 1169–72', 'Overlord becomes feudal lord, 1172–85' and 'John, lord of Ireland, 1185–1216'. Chapters II–V in A. Cosgrove (ed.), *A New History of Ireland*, II, *Medieval Ireland 1169–1534.* Oxford.

Mason, E. 1990: *St Wulfstan of Worcester.* Oxford.

McNeill, T. E. 1990: 'The great towers of early Irish castles'. *Anglo-Norman Studies*, XII, 99–117.

Meirion-Jones, G. and Jones, M. 1993: *Manorial Domestic Buildings in England and Northern France.* London.

Orpen, G. H. 1911–20: *Ireland under the Normans, 1169–1333.* 4 vols, Oxford.

Painter, S. 1933: *William Marshal.* Baltimore.

Pounds, N. J. G. 1990: *The Medieval Castle in England and Wales: A Social and Political History.* Cambridge. (Paperback edn 1994.)

Pryde, G. S. (ed.) 1965: *The Burghs of Scotland.* Oxford.

Rae, E. C. 1987: 'Architecture and sculpture, 1169–1603'. In A. Cosgrove (ed.), *A New History of Ireland*, II, *Medieval Ireland 1169–1534.* Oxford.

Renn, D. F. 1968: *Norman Castles in Britain.* London. (2nd edn 1973.)

Richardson, H. G. and Sayles, G. O. 1963: *The Administration of Ireland, 1172–1377.* Dublin.

Richter, M. 1988: *Medieval Ireland, the Enduring Tradition.* London.

Ritchie, R. L. G. 1954: *The Normans in Scotland.* London.

Rowlands, I. W. 1981: 'The making of the March: aspects of the Norman settlement of Dyfed'. *Proceedings of the Battle Conference on Anglo-Norman Studies*, III, 142–57.

Sawyer, P. 1985: *Domesday Book: A Reassessment*. London.

Simpson, G. and Webster, B. 1985: 'Charter evidence and the distribution of mottes in Scotland'. In K. Stringer (ed.), *Essays on the Nobility of Medieval Scotland*. Edinburgh, 1–24.

Simpson, W. D. 1959: *Scottish Castles*. Edinburgh. (A late and short survey which summarizes his views on a number of castles.)

Spurgeon, C. J. 1987: 'Mottes and castle-ringworks in Wales'. In J. R. Kenyon and R. Avent (eds), *Castles in Wales and the Marches*. Cardiff, 23–46.

Stalley, R. A. 1971: *Architecture and Sculpture in Ireland 1150–1350*. Dublin.

Stenton, F. M. 1932: *English Feudalism 1066–1166*. Oxford. (2nd edn 1961.)

Strickland, M. (ed.) 1992: *Anglo-Norman Warfare*. Woodbridge.

Stringer, K. (ed.) 1985a: *Essays on the Nobility of Medieval Scotland*. Edinburgh.

Stringer, K. 1985b: 'The early lords of Lauderdale Dryburgh abbey and St Andrew's priory at Northampton'. In K. Stringer (ed.), *Essays on the Nobility of Medieval Scotland*. Edinburgh.

Stringer, K. 1985c: *Earl David of Huntingdon, 1152–1219: A Study in Anglo-Norman History*. Edinburgh.

Walker, D. G. 1978a: 'Cardiff'. In R. A. Griffiths (ed.), *Boroughs of Medieval Wales*. Cardiff, 103–28.

Walker, D. G. 1978b: 'The Norman settlement in Wales'. *Proceedings of the Battle Conference on Anglo-Norman Studies*, I, 131–43.

Walker, D. G. 1984: 'Cultural survival in an age of conquest'. In R. R. Davies, R. A. Griffiths, I. G. Jones, and K. O. Morgan (eds), *Welsh Society and Nationhood*. Cardiff, 35–50.

Walker, D. G. 1990: *Medieval Wales*. Cambridge.

Warren, W. L. 1961: *King John*. London. (2nd edn 1978.)

Warren, W. L. 1973: *Henry II*. London.

Watt, J. A. 1970: *The Church and Two Nations in Medieval Ireland*. Cambridge.

Watt, J. A. 1972: *The Church in Medieval Ireland*. Dublin.

Wightman, W. E. 1966: *The Lacy Family in England and Normandy, 1066–1194*. Oxford.

Index

Place-names in this index are identified by regions in Scotland and by modern shires in England, Ireland and Wales.